The Noble Edge

"*The Noble Edge* is fast paced, easy to read and covers a lot of ground. I have not seen a distinction between morals and ethics as well delineated as in this work. It's a great primer for corporate and individual social responsibility."

**Mike Phillips**, Board Chairperson, Altaira
Capital Partners Ltd., London,
Chairman and CEO, Russell Investments, Ret.

"Wow! I couldn't put it down! The book is brilliant, inspiring, filled with humor that informs and amazing personal stories. If I were still Dean of the USC Law School, I would assign it to every law student. This book has given me some GREAT material for my monthly firesides that will be duly attributed and acknowledged."

**Dorothy Nelson**, Past Dean,
University of Southern California Law School and
40-Year Member of the National Spiritual Assembly
of the Bahá'í's of the United States, Ret.

"Chris thoughtfully and purposefully guides and inspires one's capacity for nobility."

**Laurel Anderson Rostami**, MA, ABS, LMHC,
Founder, Conscious Completion

"Dr. Christopher Gilbert has delivered a much-needed tonic in an increasingly toxic moral era. His vast experiences in researching and teaching in the field of ethics, combined with his deeply held personal beliefs and seasoned practice in living out the principles he shares, combine to make *The Noble Edge* an insightful and powerful guide that will enrich us all. There's no more right time than now to sharpen the ethical lens of our lives, and this is the book that can do it!"

**Mike Yoder**, Executive Director,
Associated Ministries

"*The Noble Edge* is written with an engaging style that brought clarity to my thinking about how I live my life with the rest of the world. It moves quickly and focused my thoughts on my current behaviors."

**Frank Hagel**, President, Hagel and Company,
Human Resource Management Systems

"This book is a gift to all who read it! It's a fast and fun journey across common ethical frameworks but not from an ivory tower perspective, despite the author's clear academic foundations and solid research. It's entertaining and the examples are practical. Chris shares his life's wisdom and depth of studies to debunk many of the shaky ethical foundations we often stand on. But he doesn't leave us abandoned; he proposes a superior and viable way of ethical thinking that leads to the right kinds of actions, not only for us, but for all. Whether you're seeking growth in your personal life or within the business community, I highly recommend it to anyone who aspires to live an "examined life" and be at their very best."

**Don Sosnowski**, Executive Director,
Invista Performance Solutions

"Dr. Gilbert has written an engaging and insightful book that is both grounded in theory and immensely practical. It culminates in nine steps that support each of us in reaching the ethical high ground, and along the way we are treated to stories and examples that bring the material to life. Rarely does a book bring together so many important ideas and empower us to make better moral choices. Gilbert's work is an enjoyable, meaningful, accessible book for everyone."

**Dr. Jill Purdy**, Executive Vice Chancellor for
Academic Affairs, Professor of Management,
University of Washington, Tacoma

"Dr. Gilbert's unique approach to cultivating greater honesty and integrity in our lives is a must read! It provides insight, optimism and humor on the opportunity we have to change things as individuals and make a difference in our families, organizations and communities."

**Randie Gottlieb**, Ed.D., Founding Executive Director, UnityWorks Foundation

"In this very readable and practical approach to ethics, Chris Gilbert brings his years of experience, his substantial knowledge and research and his quick wit. Chris has made the topic approachable and straight forward."

**Joe Lawless**, Executive Director, Milgard Center for Leadership & Social Responsibility

"It's a known cliché that it's easier to preach moral standards rather than live by them. However, Dr. Gilbert's book will help to close the gap by showing why and how you can actually walk the talk. With the ease of a laid-back, conversational style and filled with personal anecdotes, insights from ancient wisdom and engaging case studies, this book will provide you the moral clarity to do the right thing."

**Dr. Turan Kayaoglu**, Associate Vice Chancellor for Research, University of Washington

"*The Noble Edge* offers the wisdom of the ages in a style that is deep yet easy to understand. Through a book that is both personal and professional, Dr. Gilbert has encapsulated ethical mileposts into 21 Principles of Leading an Ethically Driven Life. These nuggets of wisdom, called Moral Progressivism, help us reflect on living a truly ethical life. This book is a window into a future that will be both challenging and rewarding. Recommended reading for all sentient beings."

**Trip Barthel**, Author, *Transforming Conflict into Consensus*

"I greatly enjoyed *The Noble Edge*. The writing is lively and engaging, and the subject matter is applicable in the classroom, the boardroom and the family room. The stories within draw from Dr. Gilbert's wide range of life experience in business and education and underscore the breadth and depth of the ethical challenges we face as individuals, communities and nations. In a world increasingly awash in ethical relativism, Chris's thoughtful and straightforward analysis gives us an owner's manual for ethical behavior. This book should be a must-read for every college freshman, every corporate executive, every board member and every trustee. Ethical behavior, as Dr. Gilbert points out so clearly, is a process—one in which we are all engaged."

**Dr. Brian Duchin**, Professor of History,
Department of Social Sciences,
Tacoma College, Washington

# *The*
# NOBLE
# EDGE

*Reclaiming an Ethical World*
*One Choice at a Time*

## CHRISTOPHER
## GILBERT PhD

NEW YORK

LONDON • NASHVILLE • MELBOURNE • VANCOUVER

# The Noble Edge

## Reclaiming an Ethical World One Choice at a Time

Published in New York, New York, by Morgan James Publishing. Morgan James is a trademark of Morgan James, LLC. www.MorganJamesPublishing.com

A **FREE** ebook edition is available for you or a friend with the purchase of this print book.

CLEARLY SIGN YOUR NAME ABOVE

**Instructions to claim your free ebook edition:**
1. Visit MorganJamesBOGO.com
2. Sign your name CLEARLY in the space above
3. Complete the form and submit a photo of this entire page
4. You or your friend can download the ebook to your preferred device

ISBN 9781631954054 paperback
ISBN 9781631954061 eBook
Library of Congress Control Number: 2020949838

**Cover and Interior Design by:**
Chris Treccani
www.3dogcreative.net

Morgan James is a proud partner of Habitat for Humanity Peninsula and Greater Williamsburg. Partners in building since 2006.

Get involved today! Visit
MorganJamesPublishing.com/giving-back

*To my dearest friend, wife, and shipmate, Marie,*
*who is as constant, hopeful and selflessly giving*
*as the northern star (Go Elly!).*

# TABLE OF CONTENTS

# ACKNOWLEDGMENTS

I could not have written this book alone, and I am grateful for the many ways others contributed including (but not limited to):

My daughters, Shannon and Stephanie, who always give their best; Dr. Pattabi Raman, who launched this voyage; Laurel Anderson-Rostami, who taught me how to strive for authenticity every waking moment; Lori Wyckoff, who patiently urged me down the path of conscious knowledge; Tom and Lela Holden, who catalyzed my declaration; my parents, Liz and Paul and brothers Greg and Kevin, who always offered safe harbor in any storm; my extended family and loving community members, friends and colleagues who buoyed my hopes when life brought this subject to my front door; my crews on- and offshore who were consistently brave, perseverant and adventurous; and the encouragement and support offered by everyone who understands the true relationship between words and deeds.

And finally, to my own God-given journey toward radiant acquiescence in a world where there is no such thing as good or bad—only progress!

# INTRODUCTION

*"Empathy is about finding echoes of*
*another person in yourself."*
—Moshin Hamid

There is no right way to do the wrong thing. We spend our lives bumping up against the lessons in those words. Corporate executives of multi-billion-dollar companies who once made multi-million-dollar salaries are spending prison time with those words. Hollywood moguls and powerful politicians have been retired by those words. Spiritual leaders have been defrocked ignoring those words. Doctors, lawyers, accountants, engineers, educators, community leaders, sports and entertainment stars, you, me, our children—no one escapes them.

They are simple. They are essential. They are the quality we make of our lives. And they are needed now, more than ever.

As an international ethics consultant and "seasoned" university professor, I feel my job is to start a conversation about what it means to do right in business and in life despite the constant personal, social, economic and other cultural and societal pressures to ignore what is "right" in favor of "success." Face it: our world highly rewards individual initiative and holds in high esteem a winner defined largely by his or her title, possessions and popularity—not a very good footing for strong or consistent ethical choice-making.

Over the years, I've learned a lot in both researching and teaching ethics. For one, I have come to realize that my students predictably and regularly have what I call *"ethics out-of-body experiences."* That is, they seem to share the notion that, while they are reading about those "awful and evil people" who make unethical decisions defrauding millions, they themselves could not or would not ever make such bad choices.

I try to explain that poor choices are often made with the firm belief they are good choices, not unethical or even illegal ones. After all, no business leader making a bad choice walks into the corporate board room and queries, "All those in favor of making a terrible decision that hurts our consumers but makes us a lot of money, please raise your hands!" Unethical decisions rarely, if ever transpire that way. Instead, poor choices are often rationalized and supported by some belief that ultimately justifies them as best— even when others may get hurt as a result.

As my students examine the stories I share with them about well-known, failed leaders who ultimately believed there is a right way to do the wrong thing, I am struck by the gap between their erroneous belief in their own ethical infallibility and their everyday actions. As we chat, they rather consistently demonstrate they see no incongruity in distancing themselves from the ethically-flawed corporate executives they could never become. They do this, even as some of them are downloading illegally-posted movies and copyrighted software off the internet, plagiarizing bits of published articles to write a better paper, completing work covertly for their schoolmates, deceiving loved ones about their relationships and on and on.

## Who Me, Unethical?

This is the "ethics-out-of-body experience"—judging others with a different set of lenses than we use to judge ourselves. It is the common act of standing apart from our own ability to make the bad choices we rationalize as right, even as we read about the bad choice-makers caught in public scandals who do exactly the same thing, only on a bigger scale.

And it's not just my students. I see this same unspoken attitude while giving ethics trainings, keynotes and presentations around the world. Whether it's corporate boards, doctors, lawyers, accountants, government officials, educational institutions, non-profit organizations or international conferences, I will often jokingly ask, "Will everyone who's come to this talk today because they're unethical, please raise your hands?" Not surprisingly, no hands appear. "That's right." I respond, "You aren't worried about you, because you live by the highest standards. It's that person on your left and your right you're concerned about. Who's glad those folks came to this presentation today?" At that point, all hands go up.

How is this possible? Sometimes people's rationale is that they are "better" people. Sometimes their rationale is that small choices such as illegal downloads or plagiarizing or skipping out of work don't really hurt anyone the same way as financial fraud or job discrimination. Sometimes the rationale is that they're too smart to get caught. All this to say, whether it is millions of stolen dollars, a few stolen days of unearned time off, or a few stolen words lifted from some dusty journal, being ethical is being ethical and being unethical is being unethical.

Claiming you can be "sort of" ethical because it's only hurting a few is like claiming you are sort of pregnant. Sorry, the fact is you either are or you are not. That's what we look for from our ethics— a solid right and a solid wrong. Now, don't misunderstand me. There are a lot of situations where the circumstances make things so grey it's hard to see right from wrong. But that's our perception. As I will explain in this book, there is always a right and wrong to every decision that affects others. The question is, how clearly do we want to see it? And when we do see it, what are we willing to do about it?

## The Noble Edge —Toward a Better Future

My corporate training events and university courses showed me quickly that we needed a different conversation about ethics and moral decision-making. We needed something that would cut through this erroneous belief that bad ethics are practiced by bad people and good ethics come from the rest of us.

What's the bottom line? Why read another book about the good, the bad and the waffly?

I offer this humble edict: we can either work together to create a healthy morality and ethics that treat *everyone* with equity and justice at all times. Or you can put this book down, and keep believing in the situational ethics where some of us are treated more fairly than others some of the time and being treated with compassion and empathy is the luck of the draw. You can either believe we have the capacity to create a world that supports consistent good-choice-making, or you can continue believing all ethics are arbitrary, and can change from time to time, place to place and person to person. I passionately request you and I choose the former world and not the latter.

That's our mission—one of the purposes of life. To walk consistently toward the Noble Edge.

What's the Noble Edge?

You are probably familiar with the competitive edge, the cutting edge and the leading edge. These refer symbolically to those rarified spaces in business and science and life, where brand new ideas, new technologies, new ways of thinking and acting spur incredible, sometimes unpredictable innovations and advances.

The Noble Edge represents an advance in our character.

This is the space where the nobility we are born with flourishes through the agreement of our words and deeds. A place where honesty and integrity always underscore our ethical choices.

The climb there requires wit and wisdom as we struggle to balance our own desires with the recognition of our impacts on others. But the view from the edge is empowering! Astounding!!

Living at the Noble Edge brings a consistency to our values and our virtues. It presents us a vista of the complete transformation in our relationships which have always thrived on trust and trustworthiness.

This book offers researched, tangible proof we can create more unifying, more profitable and more livable ethics one choice at a time. We have the amazing power to reclaim an ethical world despite the near daily challenges to our trust. And this journey toward the Noble Edge starts with a different type of conversation than we've had before. This book seeks to open that conversation.

# CRISIS AND VICTORY!

## *The Compassion of Ethics*

*"There is no such thing as a problem without a gift for you in its hands.*
*You seek problems because you need their gifts."*
—*Richard Bach,* Illusions

Never underestimate the progress offered by a crisis. If we could see the end of the pathway from its beginnings, we would relish the inevitable victories offered in our stumbling's and setbacks. Take for example, the improbable journey that led to me writing this book.

I did not start off my career with a Ph.D. specializing in leadership ethics. In fact, I first earned a Bachelor's degree in geology and then went on to an MBA in marketing, long before I met up with my real passion: ethics and human moral development.

After freezing as an engineering geologist on Alaska's North Slope for three years and then warming up as a university business professor and consultant for the following three, by the fall of 1986 I was president and partner in an entrepreneurial venture in the food business. That in itself seems an improbable journey, but the best is yet to come.

Our new business, *Cravings*, employed 35 great people working in two offices. With over a million and a half dollars of investment, we were pioneering an idea whose time has still not yet come— home delivery of nutritious, high-quality food, hot and ready to eat and available in any location you desire in thirty minutes or less, all for the same price as a large pizza.

The four of us who started *Cravings* had finally figured out why pizza was about all any of us can get delivered. We saw huge profits and great service in serving tasty, healthy foods that would better feed a wider audience than the limited and unhealthy pizza delivery market. There was finally something better than "Italian à la Cardboard!" We were lucky. We were skilled. And we knew the right questions to ask about the real problem.

It started with a simple question you can still ask anybody: "Do you want more than pizza delivered to your home or office?" Over 89 percent of folks asked this question will respond, "YES!" Try it yourself; ask anyone and tally the results.

That was the easy question. The harder one was why. Why aren't established pizza delivery companies trying to satisfy this huge 89 percent demand for greater variety in every city and state of the Union? Imagine the profits they would reap if they did! *We did!* Months of research gained us the answer and a few more months got us the right solution. It's all about the delivery.

As it turns out, pizza companies cannot vary their menus beyond pizza, breadsticks and salads because of the way they deliver. Personal cars delivering food out of a pizza kitchen limits delivery distance to about five miles. If they want to serve more pizza delivery customers, they must invest in building, equipping and operating a new, entirely redundant pizza kitchen that serves the next five miles. Then, they build another for the next and another for the next and so on, until the city is covered. In a city the size of Seattle in 1989, that turned out to be 36 expensive, high rent pizza stores—for just one pizza chain.

But it gets more expensive. No matter how many orders each store gets, because the pizza is cooling off while bouncing around in the back seat of the delivery car, they can only accomplish about three and a half deliveries before the car has to toddle back to the pizza store to pick up its next order of hot pizzas. That, too, limits the number of deliveries one car can make during any shift.

It gets even worse—if a pizza cools down while sliding around in a box riding in that delivery car, imagine—if they varied their menu—what your favorite seafood dish, or vegetarian plate, or fancy-sauce pasta would taste like by the time it reached your dinner plate the same way. No, pizza is about the only thing that survives such a delivery environment relatively intact and mostly edible.

There's one final fatal flaw: most people order pizza only for lunch or dinner. Imagine if you could serve breakfast, or hot cookies and milk at midnight or a burger and fries after the bars close? Truly, pizza doesn't meet our needs by any stretch of the imagination. These reasons and more are why pizza delivery is still just pizza delivery more than three and a half decades after we opened *Cravings*.

Why am I talking about pizza delivery in a book about right and wrong decisions? Because in this story, the crisis that urged me down an ethics pathway is about to explode. Read on . . .

**Risky Business**

By 1989, we had successfully operated *Cravings*—our innovative hot meal delivery company—for three years. We proved that our technology worked and the profits were real. We were ready for more investment to get our operation out of a small test market in Bellingham, Washington and into Seattle (our hometown). Then it was on to Denver to prove winter snow couldn't stop us, and Atlanta to see how much we'd have to vary our Northwest menu for Southern tastes.

We needed money—lots of money—about three million dollars for each city. But since our business brought in plenty of cash, it was a safe, lucrative investment. For next-level funding, we approached large food makers including General Mills, Quaker Oats, Proctor and Gamble, Heinz, Simplot, Con Agra, and others (about 20 others). Four of these companies wanted details of our operation and two of them began negotiating a deal to provide us expansion capital. In fact, these two companies sent representatives out to our test site to see for themselves how it all worked.

It was risky to let executives from huge potential competitors see our operations (now that's an interesting commentary on current business ethics all by itself). But because of Black Monday in October of '89, a major stock market adjustment, there was little private, venture capital money available anywhere. So, we had little choice but to approach the big kahunas. Of course, we had them sign legal agreements, specifically Non-Compete (legalese for "You can't steal our idea") and Non-Disclosure (legalese for "Even if you don't want to buy it, you can't sell our idea to anybody").

After having us sign the same documents, each of our potential buyers spent about a month at our test site investigating us. The fancy name for this process is "due diligence"—coming to understand all aspects of a business before risking any money on it. One company was so pleased after its initial due diligence that it immediately began negotiating to provide us the expansion money. The other big-name firm went silent for about a month, until we received a letter from their lawyers telling us they were no longer interested in food delivery. They were opting instead to compete with the new Healthy Choice line of frozen foods and lunch meats that their multi-billion-dollar competitor, Con Agra, had just successfully introduced to the marketplace. I guess they saw more profit in sandwiches!

So far, so good. Now for the explosion.

As we were negotiating with the other big-name food company, (I'll call them FoodX), we learned that the sandwich lovers who had turned us down had opened an operation exactly like ours in a "hidden" test market in Eden Prairie, Minnesota. In fact, they'd spent around four million dollars to open *Bringers*. What a name! *Bringers* used the same general menu, same delivery vehicles, same kitchen technologies, same ordering methods and same marketing angles as *Cravings*.

We immediately flew out to Minnesota to confirm our worst fears. Sure enough, *Bringers* was real and basically a carbon copy of our company. Sandwiches, my butt! These guys had taken our ideas and technologies and gone into food delivery after all!

Our immediate reaction was to sue. After all, we had signed agreements to prevent this very circumstance. But this was literally out of the question. How could we afford the legal team needed to take on this multi-billion-dollar food giant that had stolen our idea, especially when this company had banks of lawyers that would keep their *Bringers* moving forward for years while we withered away under court costs? No, suing wasn't a realistic option. There would be no David and Goliath story here. *Bringers* would live on.

After that sorrowful realization, we were faced with the real ethical challenge: would we tell FoodX, the company still negotiating with us, about *Bringers* secret test marketing? We knew full well FoodX was mainly interested in us because we were their best opportunity to be first into any home delivery market in the U.S. With *Bringers* up and running, that was no longer true. *Bringers* could open everywhere sooner because it had already launched and had lots of money behind it.

**So, here's the first ethical quandary of this book: would you tell FoodX about *Bringers*, knowing they will almost certainly back out of a multi-million-dollar deal with you?**

The reality here is that if FoodX funds your expansion, your company grows and you personally get rich. If they back out from the deal, your company closes and you and your 35 employees are laid off by the early investors who funded your start-up in order to reap the profits of a big buy-out.

What would you do?

Fortunately, our team knew that there's no right way to do the wrong thing. After little debate, including conversations with all of our employees, we gave FoodX all of the information about *Bringers*.

Boom!

Explosion!!

Layoffs!!!

*Cravings kaput!!!!*

And as FoodX bowed out of the deal and our investors closed us down, we were left with nothing of value to anyone else except a few ovens and the truth.

And me? I was left standing at a crossroads: would I jump into some other entrepreneurial adventure, or was there a deeper lesson in this *Cravings* crisis that begged to be explored? As you can see, I chose exploration.

I put my efforts and energies into the study of ethics and human morality, traveling and working on four different continents for over 25 years. I realized two important things in that journey. First, if I wanted to talk with any authority about something as personal, and dare I say, as dangerous as our human ability to make unethical choices, I needed to do some research. And second, I'd need to get my doctorate. After all, if I was going to call myself an ethics sheriff, I'd better have my boots, holster, and hat. So, in 2002, wanting to find a better way to teach, train, and speak about this crucial subject, I plunged into a six-year journey to obtain my Ph.D. If you haven't already guessed it, there was of course another reason hiding in my growing passion to discover the secret of more consistent ethical choice-making: *Cravings*. Executives at that powerful, sandwich-loving food company had stolen our ideas, our company and our lives. How much more unethical can you get in the business world?

## Defining Ethics

Before I venture further down this path, I believe it will be useful to agree on working definitions of some basic ethics-speak, in the hope it will lay a common ground for ideas shared in this book.

These are terms my research clearly defined for me and I trust they will be valuable to my readers, as well.

**In the broadest context, an ethical choice is any decision or action that has an impact on others now or in the future.** Face it, apart from possible future environmental impacts, it's hard to make an unethical choice living alone on a desert island. Our ethics affect others and theirs in turn affect us.

## The Difference between Morals, Ethics, and Legality[1]

> *"Morals are in the talking—ethics are in the acting!"*
> **-DR. BILL GRACE, Center for Ethical Leadership**

**Morals** are the standards of an individual or group about what is right and what is wrong.

**Ethics** are an examination of right and wrong and the actions taken after that examination.

**Legality** (what is legal or illegal) comes from enforced social arrangements based on our morals.

**Moral development** is the continual growth of moral reasoning and moral capacity. Dr. Lawrence Kohlberg and his associates at Harvard's Center for Moral Education identified three distinct levels and six stages of this development starting in 1976 (more about this later).

**Ethical development** is the progression of actions based on an increasingly selfless perspective in our decisions.

Here's the surprise about invoking the legal or illegal question to judge ethical behavior (which is common practice in business): legality is the low bar where moral conversations start and ethical actions begin. "Legal "or "illegal" is the *beginning* of the discussion about ethics, not the *end*. Even the law changes to reflect our social moral development.

Consider the egregious segregation and inequality laws that separated people of color and kept women from voting in this country. As our capacity grows, so does our understanding of the universal nature of equity, equality and morality. This is reflected over time in changes

---

1    For a deeper treatment of these definitions, see "Expanded Definitions" in Appendix A at the back of this book.

to our laws. In essence, changing laws reflect our moral progression as individuals and as a society.

• • • • • • • • • • • • • • • • • • • • • • • • • • • • • • • • • • •

## INSTANT REPLAY

**Morals**: the standards of an individual or group about what is right and wrong

**Ethics**: the examination of right and wrong through conduct and the practice of right

**Legality**: codes of conduct that meet the minimum requirements of ethical behavior

**Moral and Ethical Development**: our capacity for growth in the selflessness of our thoughts and actions

• • • • • • • • • • • • • • • • • • • • • • • • • • • • • • • • • • •

### Grace Learns about Laws versus Ethics

 In an attempt to put all four of these definitions together in one useful example, let me introduce Grace, a fictitious person whom we'll see in and out of various ethical dilemmas throughout this book. (Say, "Hi!" Grace. Oops, she can't talk. Sorry, Grace...)

In each scenario I describe, I will tell you the moral I'm illustrating, then I'll tell you the story showing how that moral relates to Grace's situation.

## FIRE!

**The moral**: Moral standards require each of us to balance different individual rights so that we act ethically, especially in circumstances where there are no laws defining our actions as legal or illegal.

**The scenario**: Grace is about to yell, "Fire!" in a crowded theater to see people's reactions. Without thinking much about it, she is relying on a moral standard to do this: freedom of choice. She knows the First Amendment; Freedom of Speech is supporting her. But while Grace is utilizing one moral standard about a choice for herself, she is ignoring others' right to choose—in this case, their right to choose to live in safety.

It turns out, unhappily for Grace, there is a law against this very thing. *The Clear and Present Danger Laws* prohibit anyone from creating a potential danger, such as this one, to others. Perhaps it goes without saying, but the danger here is caused by Grace willfully inciting panic in a crowded room with a lie. If Grace goes through with this, she is acting both illegally, because she breaks the law, and unethically because, illegal or not, she'll be putting others at grave risk.

*The Clear and Present Danger Laws* were written in 1919 following the not-so-famous Supreme Court Case Schenck v. United States. Before then, the only thing stopping Grace, besides her conscience, were the moral standards that prohibit lying and unnecessarily risking others' lives.

What if Grace yells, "Fire!" in a crowded theater in 1918, the year before the law is written? Same deal: while this not yet illegal, it still violates these basic moral standards and is unethical.

Why did it take all the way until 1919 to write such laws? One could argue that the process of social moral development and other circumstances advanced our collective recognition that an individual's freedom of speech was not limitless; it must be tempered by a demonstrated concern for other's well-being.

If I'm going to stop Grace from yelling, maybe the quickest way to do so is quoting Supreme Court Justice, Oliver Wendell Holmes, who advanced our moral understanding in helping to create this law. He wrote, "Your right to swing your arms ends just where the other man's nose begins." If you take his meaning.

Ahhh, Grace is sitting back down to quietly watch the movie now. There's nothing better than some Oliver Wendell Holmes to cut through an ethical dilemma.

> ***Ethics Principle No. 1: Laws tell us what we can do; ethics tell us what we should do.***

## Our Collective Moral Development

Let me provide a more recent example of our collective moral development. Here are two actual sentences taken from IBM (the big computer company) employee manuals:

1. "Secretaries, who should all be pert, clever young women, should exemplify the best manners in pleasing bosses."

2. "The employees of IBM represent a talented and diverse workforce. Achieving the full potential of this diversity is a business priority that is fundamental to our competitive success. A key element in our workforce diversity programs is IBM's long-standing commitment to equal opportunity."

I'm sure you can guess which phrase is from 1962 and which is from 2017. Yes, that's right, number 1 is early Neanderthal and number 2 is the more recent and enlightened. In fact, when number 2 was written, the CEO of IBM was Ginni Rometti, a very capable and successful woman.

It probably goes without asking, but if you were employed by IBM, which manual would you want them to be enforcing? This difference in our understanding of the equality between men and women then and now reflects our social moral development—in this case, an evolution over 50 years or so. While the laws on women and minority rights appeared over this time, they didn't cause our moral development—our moral development caused them.

There are myriad examples of how our moral development creates or changes our laws, and how our laws enforce that change after it happens. The end of segregation, equal rights acts and fair wage laws are but a few examples. These laws reflect our social moral development.

I am reminded of a comedian's commentary about this.

A young man walks into a drugstore in the 1950s, goes up to the counter and says loudly enough for others to hear, "Give me a pack of Marlboros!" He wants to demonstrate his coolness to everyone. But then he leans in and quietly whispers to the druggist, "And I'll take a small package of condoms." Flash forward to the 2000s. Another young man, same age, walks into a drugstore goes up the counter and proudly says to the druggist, "Give me a package of those condoms!" He then leans in to whisper, "And I'll take a pack of Marlboros." Public pressure and acceptable habits have certainly changed!

Law didn't change how we think or feel about cigarettes and condoms. Our attitudes and moral behaviors changed and altered the laws about smoking and a more common acceptance of birth control.

Another thought about this process of change can provide an important perspective on the sources for our moral standards. After all, these standards define whether we are ethical or unethical in our actions. So where do we get our moral standards? Some would argue that it's rooted in ancient wisdom and philosophy, but I question the relevance of thousand-year-old perspectives in answering the complex, ethical problems of today. Don't get me wrong; I'm not knocking 7,000+ years of written debate about right and wrong. Aristotle, Plato, Socrates, Hippocrates, Archimedes—the whole "Ees" family—bring a lot to the table concerning good and bad choices and their effects on others. This is great root stock for our perspectives. But it is not the whole plant.

The capacities of these ancient philosophers and scientists were shaped by their own society's moral development as far back as 2,500 years ago. That is relevant to their vision of human rights and moral obligations. As farsighted as these great men were, and as much as they contributed to our moral standards today, they lived in tolerance of slavery, gender oppression, racial prejudice and a host of other inequities. No, if I were creating moral standards that encompass our capacities to progress, I would not rely solely on the ancient philosophers, just as I would not reference IBM's 1962 human resources manual for gender equity issues.

So where do I go to source a more progressive understanding of morality that matches our greater capacities? How do you use all the fancy terms and definitions to understand your or others' ethical actions? Is it someone's feelings or their principles that tell us about their moral code? Is an ethical choice about your motives, your intentions, or the outcomes of your actions? Is knowing the right thing to do about the impact on the individual or the community? Do we look at the long term or the short term consequences to examine the ethics of our actions?

These are all great questions. We'll have to tackle them and many others one at a time to sort this out. And on that note, let's start by looking at the ethics of language with another true story.

# WHERE'S MY DECODER RING?

## *The Language of Ethics*

*"The difference between a cat and a lie is the cat has only nine lives."*
*—Mark Twain*

About the same time that I was teaching my first ethics course at the University of Washington in 2000, ENRON was hitting the news. For those who may not remember, ENRON, a huge energy trading company in the '90s, wound up defrauding stockholders of hundreds of millions of dollars and destroying tens of thousands of employee jobs overnight. In a word, they cheated and got caught.

Without a long analysis of ENRON's foibles, company leaders essentially fooled everyone into believing the company was making money when it was not. Even the accountants and auditing firms didn't detect the fraud. In fact, some of these watchdogs were complicit in

ENRON's ability to lie to us. Someone should have yelled, "Fire!" in that theater!

How does a publicly visible company being tracked by major financial markets steal billions while everyone's watching? Part of the answer is the human ability to stop weighing what's ethical and what's not, especially if there are personal benefits in not judging. After all, why would any company blow the whistle on a very lucrative, major client? I am reminded of the Upton Sinclair quote, "It is difficult to get a man to understand something when his salary depends on his not understanding it." The same goes for women, I assume.

Another part of the answer to this question lies in lies—in particular, what ethicists (those who study ethics) label as *coded language*. All of us use coded language. It's how we pass information or ideas quickly or say something to someone in a more sensitive way. Most of the time it is not used for some nefarious and unethical purpose. We all speak in Codes.

A casual greeting such as, "Hi, how are you?" when you sweep past someone in a hallway is coded language. This greeting is rarely a question requiring a lengthy conversation about health and well-being. In our culture, these words simply mean, "Hi," or "Good day," and both parties who share this Code move on.

On the flip side, I had the opportunity of living in Pskov, Russia for a year in 1994. This repeatedly exposed me to what it's like to not share Codes. (Sounds like a spy drama, doesn't it?) I knew just enough Russian language then to be dangerous, starting with *Privyet* (Pree-vee-et, "Hello") and *Kok Dela* (Kahk-deh-lah, "How are you?"). So, as was my custom, early in my stay I would greet my Russian comrades each morning with *"Privyet, kok dela?"* At which point, they would go into several minutes of explanation about their and their family's health and well-being! (You can see me struggling to keep my pace walking down the hallway, can't you?) The bottom line is that they didn't share our Code and I didn't share theirs.

*Their* Code tells them the question is genuine and requires a genuine answer. They were often surprised by my greeting, but grateful for my concern. (They were probably hoping for a quick Russian "Hello," so they could also move on!)

## The Dark Side of Coded Language

While my foreign *faux pas* is not an example of the willing or unethical misuse of coded language, there are times when our language does have an unethical intent. We can break the shared code rules a number of ways. One of the most pervasive misuses is using language that gives the listener a small portion, but not all of what we want them to know about something. This is called a *lie of omission*, but we'll stick with the broader coded language label for now.

Here is a quick personal example. Let's say Grace is one of my students and she drops off a late assignment.

She uses the excuse that her printer ran out of ink. This sounds reasonable, so she's hoping I accept the late assignment with her excuse and grade it equally with the on-time papers. After all, how is she responsible for not knowing an opaque printer ink cartridge was running dry?

But what if Grace's printer ran out of ink three weeks earlier and she was aware of it then? Running out of ink is not the accident she portrays it to be. Although her language is communicating one fact of many—her printer did run out of ink—she omits the rest. It turns out that Grace actually watched sports over the weekend and was using extra time to complete this assignment. The Code inside her words tells me she had no control of her circumstances and should not be penalized. The truth inside her words is that the inkless printer is not the cause of the late paper—Grace's poor time management is.

I know the language one way, and she uses the language another way to her advantage. It is not to her advantage to admit to the inkless three weeks, the weekend sports binging or her procrastination. Again, the printer running out of ink is the truth, but it is what I call the "small t-truth," because it is not the whole story. The whole truth, or "capital T-Truth," includes the other circumstances. With the capital T-Truth, I could grade Grace's work by the same standards I have promised every student in the class. Late papers lose points. With coded language (small t-truth), Grace can assure that I grade her work favorably. This is an inequity for everyone involved. Even Grace loses here, as the best learning for her might be the consequences of her laziness. After all, better to learn those in school with grade points than at a job where the procrastination could bring far more severe remedies.

Another type of coded language is *misdirection*. This is deliberately using the Code to say one thing while knowing you mean something entirely different. The ENRON story is full of misdirection in coded language—it was their method of substituting small t-truth for capital T-Truth. On the surface, it appeared ENRON was complying with laws regarding financial transparency. They were communicating the information they were required to; they were just using a different Code than we were. Essentially, ENRON executives were using financial language one way and hoped we were understanding it another way. We did!

In financial terms, they called actual losses "gains." They were hiding failures in one part of the company by selling them to other parts of the company and then qualifying the losses as profits. They were also booking actual revenue from ideas that had never been put into operation under the premise that the promise of the idea had value in the bank. It was an enormous shell game, much like a giant Ponzi scheme that finally caught up to them.

If you'll allow, instead of using fancy financial talk, let me provide a more commonplace example of how ENRON misdirected us. Their communication to the world about their financial results was something akin to me appearing on a stage and announcing that I just had my beloved dog put to sleep. For you listeners, we share a strong Code in those words that is different than the words themselves. The Code tells us all this is a sad day and my dog is gone.

But what if I am misdirecting your attention? What if I use these exact words to get you to think one thing while I am actually saying another? What if my dog is not gone, because the words "put him to sleep" are meant to be taken literally, not in Code? What if the whole truth is that I took my dog to the vet, where it received a shot to help it sleep well overnight, and now it's up and dashing around better than ever? See, I had my dog put to sleep!

Similarly, ENRON counted on our interpretation of their words according to a strongly shared financial Code. Essentially, they gained an advantage from illegal transactions that we would not see as illegal because we shared the Code a different way. If you want the more technical terms, ENRON falsified its accounts, assigning losses to "unconsolidated partnerships" and near-worthless assets to "special purpose entities" with names like *Raptors, Death Star*, and *Myass*. Their misdirection ensured that their tremendous debts were seen by the financial markets as independent business firms agreeing to absorb ENRON's losses as investments. The bottom line: huge losses became huge profits in their reports to us.

What makes this lack of ethics even more insidious is that through this misdirection ENRON could claim they told us the truth and we just misunderstood. By law, they are only required to use certain words and categories; they are not legally required to determine how people interpret those words. From ENRON's perspective, they were able to convince themselves and us that they had fulfilled their financial obligations and told us what we needed to know about them. Their financial language was accurate, but the interpretation was far different from the capital T-Truth that language is set up to provide. They put their dog to sleep—a classic case of misdirection.

Codes are strong!

## Let's Get Personal

The ENRON example, while very real, is a bit "businessy" and technical. Perhaps it is worth personalizing some coded language that is more common and a little closer to home.

Have you ever shopped with your significant other (or a friend or family member) when they are trying on different clothes? They come skipping out of the dressing room, obviously happy with their choice and all you see is some hideous new outfit on them. Then comes that awful question, "Well, how do I look?"

You're in the spotlight now!

A transparent response would be something such as, "Oh, that looks hideous on you!" Or "Wow, does that make you look chubby, dear." These words convey an exact and uncoded meaning. This is transparency and transparency requires a comment that is 100 percent accurate—in this case, trying to get the questioner to immediately doff and discard the new outfit.

On the other hand, there is probably an important relationship here and *feelings do matter*. Transparency isn't always the ethical path. So, out comes the coded language. We use it all the time and it can be important. In this case, this might be a response such as, "Well, what an amazing shade of red that is, dear. I've never seen you wearing something that red before." Or perhaps you answer, "I'm not sure that outfit will fit the occasion you're buying it for." Or "I think that style always makes people look shorter than they are, don't you?" In these comments, we are hoping our listener will understand the unspoken Code so we don't have to be direct or transparent.

What's the ethical response to the question, "How do I look?" Not so fast! It's not that easy. Being ethical can take work.

There are a host of questions to answer before we can provide that ethical response.

First, why is this person asking the question? Is he or she looking for your real opinion? Is he looking for support for his choice? Is she looking to be dissuaded from buying something she's iffy about? Or is he looking to be persuaded towards something he initially didn't like, but might if you do?

Next, what do you know about fashion? How does your view fit his (or hers)? Do you have a history of picking clothing for this person? Does he or she pick your clothing?

Unfortunately, we can't always take the time to determine all of this in the moment. After all, we also share the Code that a delay in response to the question, "How do I look?" by posing another question, such as, "Why are you asking me?" or "Do you want the truth?" . . . that IS the response. The Code of more questions is the answer, "You don't like it!" Codes are important, powerful and fraught with peril, especially when we are not sharing them.

From an ethics perspective, it's best to solve these mysteries long before you're in the fitting room. It's a way to share the Code before you use it. Even then, it's possible there are other unspoken motives in looking for the answer to that thorny question, "How do I look?" The fact is, what do I know about fashion or the clothes someone else likes to wear? I have a certain perspective but frankly, my perception comes from my own likes and dislikes. Sometimes, I am not even sure why I like or dislike a certain look. And these may not be your likes or dislikes. If you're asking me so you can understand more about my preferences or, in order to look attractive to me, we should share that before the question gets asked. If we don't share this Code ahead of time, we rely on other Codes in both the question and the answer, Codes that we may or may not have in common.

(By the way, I can't tell you how many individuals come up to me after my presentations on this subject and jokingly ask, "Well, how do you think this outfit makes *me* look?" To quote Sargent Shultz, the German officer in that decades-old TV comedy, *Hogan's Heroes*, "I know nussing!")

**Ethics Principle No. 2: Transparency isn't always on the most ethical pathway, truth is.**

## Transparency versus Truthfulness

Managers, coaches, teachers, doctors, lawyers, religious leaders, executives, boards of directors, parents, friends and so many others struggle wittingly and unwittingly with the differences between being transparent and being truthful. Transparency argues for 100 percent raw truth. Truth be known, (no pun intended), there are times when raw information, while honest, may have a more destructive impact than the truth. This seems ethically counterintuitive, but perhaps a few more examples can shed some light.

As adults, we know information about the love between parents and the processes of procreation should be gently given to our children as they mature. We share bits and pieces that, while not transparent, are truthful to the level of their understanding. We might even answer their very pointed questions or observations with skillful tact that is not 100 percent raw truth. This is ethical. We share this moral code with most cultures around the world. The physics of procreation require certain levels of mature perspective—oh, you know what I mean with this coded language, right?

Let's jump to a group of executives or a board of directors who are discussing the option of layoffs to keep their company in business. The principle of 100 percent transparency argues that they share their conversations about these possible outcomes with the workers. The result, however, might be panic among those workers who, fearing downsizing, jump ship early and actually cause the whole company to founder.

These are unwarranted results from raw information—less than useful, even destructive outcomes caused by unregulated transparency. The movie *The Invention of Lying* is a comedic way to look at dozens of examples of the difference between truth-telling and transparency. The movie erroneously equates the two, but it's a fun watch.

Everyone needs time to analyze and weigh alternatives. The greater the potential impacts from the decision, often the more time required to find a good balance between truth and transparency. The problem with transparency is that the listener may not know or even want to know the difference between the process of weighing alternatives and a decision. In this case, the talk of possible layoffs becomes, through speculation and self-protection, the actual decision to lay off. We often look at others' choices about us through lenses focused on what is in our best interest.

The board and executives are responsible for all stakeholders. They are ethically obligated to weigh the diverse outcomes of the whole in making the right choices. It is therefore ethical to allow them the necessary process time. Their ethical obligation is informing stakeholders where they are in their process and releasing a decision at the moment everyone's right to that information can be respected. In this circumstance, a truthful answer to the question, "Will there be layoffs?" might be, "We are consulting about all possibilities, including layoffs and a variety of less devastating outcomes. We should be announcing the chosen path within x-amount of time. We will definitely keep you updated through this process."

## Communication Is Key

The cautionary tale here is how important sharing Codes is to communication, especially as we share the rationale for our actions. **We must be truthful in what we say and we must be transparent about the Code we're using to say it.** Where we don't share the Code we tend to fill the vacuum by trying to adopt the Codes we know to the uncertainty of what's being communicated. This doesn't usually work so well.

I learned this in real time when I had the privilege of working in Kenya, Africa multiple times starting in 2013, working on a ground-breaking, sustainable food security project with the Bill and Melinda Gates Foundation. We were creating an educational program for small-holder agribusiness entrepreneurs. It was a fabulous experience and at the end of each day I could actually say, "I helped solve world hunger today!" I'd always wanted to say that.

One of my many in-country experiences was driving. We made major road trips across that developing nation conducting surveys and examining working projects in food and livestock production. As we drove the dusty, pock-marked, asphalt and dirt roads, I was fascinated by the Kenyan road signs.

*Maasai Dairy Milk Collection Station, Kajiado town, Kenya, 2013*

This was another experience that jogged my thinking (literally and figuratively) about how important understanding Codes is to ethics and living well with others. Without turning this into a Kenyan driving test, let me provide two quick examples of how not sharing a Code leads us to fill in blanks with our own codes.

In the illustrations below are two Kenyan highway signs. What do you think they say?

Before I provide the answers, it's worth highlighting, if you didn't know the Code, that you probably tried to examine the shape of the sign, wondered about its color and even defined the unknown words using your own Code to make meaning. Let's see how you did.

The first sign was warning of a location on the road where a fatal accident has occurred in the past. *The Black Spot* refers to evil or bad juju there. This is somewhat like the roadside crosses and shrines placed by loved ones here in the U.S. to memorialize the accident sites of their beloved.

The second sign was telling you to use caution, literally to slow down, go easy. "Pole-pole" (polee-polee) is a Masai phrase used commonly to justify taking your time to finish something. It's a bit like being on what our Code calls "island-time." Are you ready to drive the Kenyan roads?

This example illustrates the fact that truth requires more than the right words; it requires we share the meaning behind our words—our Codes. This is as true of the emotional codes in your words as it is in the literal and figurative meaning of them. As we've already examined, the more emotion-laden or grave the impact of our actions, the more important it is we communicate the Codes in our language. This means not only using the right words, but ensuring our listeners understand what we say and the way we mean it.

Whose responsibility is it to share the Code? It's the responsibility of both the sender and the receiver. There can be plenty of hidden agendas on either side of a conversation. The more they hide and the less you seek AND the more you hide and the less they seek, the sooner the ethical game is over.

What is the commonality in these examples? The capacity of the listener.

> *Ethics Principle No. 3: Questions with a listening ear will get you a lot closer to the truth than creating your own.*

• • • • • • • • • • • • • • • • • • • • • • • • • • • • • • • • •

## INSTANT REPLAY

**Coded Language**: truthful communication of words, symbols, sounds and body language when sender and receiver share their actual and symbolic meanings

**Lies of Omission**: exclusionary detailing, omitting facts and/or failing to correct misconceptions

**Misdirection**: knowledgably incorrect, misguiding, or misleading communication

**"Small t-truth"**: a belief or paradigm that captures only a portion or none of the whole truth

**"Capital T-Truth"**: a belief or paradigm that captures the whole truth

**Transparency**: communication that transmits 100 percent fact or opinion without rational or emotional filters

**Stakeholders**: all those who will be affected now or in the future by an ethical choice

• • • • • • • • • • • • • • • • • • • • • • • • • • • • • • • • • • • •

## The Potentials of Truth and Transparency

Let's allow Grace to help us review the ethics of trust and transparency.

We empower our doctors with the duty of informing us about both the positive and negative results in diagnoses of our health. In a worst-case scenario, this may be discovering and explaining a fatal disease. Many would argue that if a doctor suspects a patient has a limited time to live, he or she should provide that information to the patient immediately so that the patient and everyone in his or her life can prepare themselves. But there may be a fatal flaw in a blanket policy of 100 percent transparency in any diagnosis. This may not be the most ethical path.

Consider this: firstly, doctors do not always have a 100 percent accurate diagnosis. No, there are many examples of health conditions, even fatal ones, that were diagnosed one way and patients lived a long and healthy life despite the deadly forecast. Secondly, we know so little about the effects our human psyches have on our health and lifespans. In other words, a premature, fatal diagnosis may create its own self-fulfilling psychology (i.e., if you know you're going to die because the doctor announces it, then that is what you'll do.) Is there a choice to live with a fatal diagnosis? Of course, there is. Our psychology, combined with the uncertain outcomes of every diagnosis, plus the near infinite number of ways and means to tackle illnesses, may mean the fatal diagnosis is absolutely wrong—even if in hindsight.

So, what is the ethical consideration here if it is not 100 percent transparency? Consider that a doctor is never 100 percent sure about every diagnosis. He or she relies on research statistics and experience; therefore, there is no 100 percent transparency to offer in any diagnosis unless it includes all possible alternative outcomes. In fact, total transparency in any diagnosis would have to include the uncertainty of the diagnosis itself. The more fatal the forecast, the more probabilities and possibilities would be apportioned into a 100 percent transparent diagnosis.

## One Life to Live

**The moral**: Humans are rarely 100 percent sure about any forecast. Truthfulness requires us to communicate our uncertainties and support rather than extinguish human virtues such as hope, faith, patience, and perseverance.

 **The scenario**: Grace is at the doctor and just received a terminal diagnosis. Grace's doctor wants to provide her accurate information about her deadly illness while simultaneously making her aware of the many unknowns in her prognosis.

I'm not sure we can be formulaic here, but words of positive possibility may be far more accurate and healthy than the potential inaccuracy of fatal probabilities. How about, instead of, "Grace, you have a one in ten chance of survival," or "Grace, you have just six weeks to live," the message is, "Grace, I'd rather be providing a diagnosis of full health, but it's important you know the possibilities. In some cases, what you have can be fatal. Yet, there is no 100 percent accurate diagnosis, and you have the possibility of overcoming this. It will take work on both our parts. And there is no guarantee it will be 100 percent successful. But the only way you can heal is if we work together and believe in the people who, even though they received the same diagnosis, overcame it to live long and happy lives. Shall we buck the odds? Do you want to work together toward that happier result?"

What about the worst case? What if Grace has something no one has ever recovered from? Is there a possibility she could be the first? Of course, there is. But in many parts of our current medical world, God forbid we fill her with hope.

There are myriad ways to preserve hope and speak the truth. The truth is we don't know how our rational, emotional, physical and spiritual intelligences act to heal us. We do know that hopelessness itself can kill.

In all this interpreting and sharing, I am not suggesting we always take the time to reveal all of our Codes before all of our conversations. I am merely highlighting how crucial it is that we understand we are often sharing coded language, especially in those situations that have crucial outcomes and emotional overtones.

There were definitely crucial outcomes to the years of coded financial responses from ENRON. And frankly speaking, there are definitely Codes being used and abused in high places in today's tweets and texts and other statements between nations and political parties. These Codes are covert and answers about their exact meaning seem to change from response to response. The outcome of all this obfuscation is a growing uncertainty. As I said, Codes are powerful ways to add to trustworthiness—or to erode it.

Language can be used ethically and it can be used unethically. Since communicating is action, we can examine communication using the same ethical lenses we use to examine our other actions. The bottom line: when in doubt, ask and listen. And when you're certain, ask and listen as well!

# IT'S NOT ABOUT INFORMATION; IT'S ABOUT TRANSFORMATION

## *The Clarity of Ethics*

*Many people spend too much time trying to be the
captain of someone else's boat.
Learn to be a lighthouse and the boats will find their way.*
*—Anonymous*

In the summer of 2000, I accomplished one of my major bucket list items: I skippered our forty-foot sailboat, *Crescendo*, in the Pacific Cup Race from San Francisco, California to Kaneohe, Hawaii. This race takes place over 2000 miles of open ocean, blue water sailing and we had a crew of seven souls aboard for the *17-day voyage*.

The race was fun, but it usually lasts only 10 or 11 days, so we hadn't exactly planned on more than two weeks of self-sufficiency on the wide-open sea. We drifted for nearly five days as the wind quit during the middle of the race. And while that allowed us the excitement of swimming in the 6000-foot deep waters of the mid-Pacific (a pretty eerie feeling), it didn't help us earn any trophies for the mantel at home.

Now, before you start speculating that this is a story about the ethics of cannibalism at sea after we ran out of food and water, let me assure you we all finished the race intact and well fed. No, while the race was long and becalmed, it was the earlier, six-day delivery of the boat from Seattle to San Francisco before the race that I tell of in this tale! On that portion of our journey, my crew and I faced three-and-a-half days of 40 to 50 knot winds (46 to 57 miles

per hour) and 20-foot breaking waves. It was, in a word, *rambunctious*. (I could use a lot of other descriptors, but that one is the most ethical.)

On the fifth day, we were sailing into the California coast from about 100 miles offshore and I could see we would reach the dangerous surf on the coastline in pitch-black, stormy conditions well after midnight. This is not a good situation for any sailor, let alone one who had no local knowledge and was unfamiliar with those shores. We decided that, instead of trying to thread our way under the Golden Gate Bridge and into San Francisco Bay at zero-dark-thirty in stormy conditions, we would opt to tuck in behind Point Reyes and anchor in Drake's Bay until sun up.

Drake's Bay is the historic landing place of Sir Francis Drake's ship, *The Golden Hind*, when he was caught in similar conditions on the 17th of June, 1579. He too was forced to take shelter there, about 25 miles north of San Francisco Bay. So, far from feeling defeated with our decision, as we dropped anchor, I felt in close kindred spirit with that 16th century buccaneer who may have moored in the exact same spot nearly 241 years earlier to the day. *But arghh, me matey, let's get back to the real story. . .*

As we headed toward the unseen shoreline, we were all exhausted, but I couldn't have been prouder. The crew had done well and the boat had done even better. No one sleeps in conditions like this. I had set the watch schedule so my most experienced crewmember, Mike, and I would be up on deck to steer us into calmer waters. As he and I climbed into the open cockpit around 1:00 a.m., it was noisy from the wind and wet from the waves, but the boat was tracking well.

As I took the helm and looked toward the bow, I could make out a white light that flashed over our heads in the roiling clouds about every five seconds. It was reflecting off an angry, black, swirling sky pelting us with rain—but it was a beacon! We were still over 20 miles away from the coastline, but this guiding beam was the Point Reyes Lighthouse telling us where we were, confirming we had gotten it right after 650 miles of ocean sailing and that we were close to getting home.

I was thankful, prayerful, thrilled, and adrenaline-rushed all at the same time! I turned to Mike, sitting in the cockpit in front of me, and shouted over the wind, "My God, am I glad to see that!"

Now, Mike can be humorous, and he can be stoic. He chose a bit of both as he yelled back over the wind, "You know Chris, that lighthouse isn't beckoning us there. It's screaming, *Whatever you do folks, don't come here!* (Wow, thanks a lot for that celebratory attitude and blinding optimism, my friend.)

His response was a bit too moribund for my joy at the time, but Mike was absolutely right. Lighthouses don't message sailors, *Come on over here, it's safe.* They shout in brazen symbols of light and dissonant symphonies of bell and horn, *This is not a safe place—go away, go far away from here!* Lighthouses sit atop rocks, cliffs, reefs, shoals, sand bars and a host of other places eager to rob a vessel of its most crucial resource: the water beneath it. Yep, Mike was right. Still, a few hours later, avoiding the nastier bits of Point Reyes itself, we were anchored in relatively calm water and sound asleep. We navigated the Golden Gate Bridge in sunshine and lightly choppy waters later that morning.

I pondered that lighthouse moment for years, wondering if there was some important but hidden lesson useful to my journey in understanding ethics. And sure enough, I finally found it. I believe the lighthouse serves as a great analogy for what ethics do for us. Like the lighthouse, ethics provide us with a reference point—enlightened guidance along the path to make the best choices for ourselves and others. They warn of danger as well.

*Ethics serve as our lighthouses.*

*Point Reyes Lighthouse, Drakes Bay, California*

My discovery in that profound sailing experience led me to think about ethics and moral development in an entirely different way. What had once been simply laws, rules, guidelines, policies and procedures, compliance, legality, philosophy, conscience and even sin now became concrete and actionable moments of good choice-making. *A study in ethics isn't about information, it's about transformation.* What I mean by that is I can create all the lighthouse moments I want, but unless I choose to use them for my own transformation, they are merely information.

*The Cambridge American Dictionary* defines "transformation" as "a complete change in the appearance or character of something or someone." As we earlier defined, the very word "ethics" comes from the Greek word *ethos* or "character." So then, we might say that a growing awareness and practice of ethics is in essence also a profound transformation of our character. This growing awareness often comes as we navigate the more dramatic or challenging events in our lives.

My old perspective had painted ethics as grey, squishy, and philosophical, born of my family and upbringing, part of my culture and religiously or academically based. Worst of all, my ethics were changeable. (Maybe you've encountered your own set of perspectives like this before. In fact, there is one ethical framework specifically justifying ethical squishiness and changeability. It's called Relativism, and we'll look at it and several other "Isms" in later chapters.)

## Trusting Our Lighthouse Moments

Some believe that ethical choices are relative to whom and what you know and when you know it. This is akin to the idea that "ignorance of the law is an excuse." If you, in your culture don't know the laws or morays of my culture, and vice versa, each of us following our own cultural laws and ethical practices is fine. This is true whether these are based on capital T-Truths of justice and equity or small t-truths of selfishness and inequity. One version of ethical choice-making claims if I am following my laws and morals and you are following yours, we are both ethical. But think about that for a minute. Do you want to come to a four-way stop sign across from a driver unfamiliar with our traffic laws who goes speeding unhesitatingly through the intersection following his or her own laws and feeling blissfully "ethical"?

After my lighthouse experience, I began to recognize that ethics, while supported by what we *know,* or where we're from are far more about what we *do,* sometimes despite what we know. It is ethics practiced on this basis that brings about our transformation. Take for example, the life-giving decision made by an organ donor. Despite what the donor knows about the grave risks associated with donating, he or she makes a profound ethical choice. I'm not suggesting we all must donate organs to be ethical. I am suggesting, that for those who might consider such a choice, the actual decision comes in a transformational moment. Ethics always come down to actions that impact others now or in the future.

> ***Ethical Principle No. 4: Our ethics are expressed not in what we say, but by what we do.***

While you may never have a literal lighthouse moment like mine, let me provide a more personalized example that has the potential of altering your perspective on ethics. Have you ever driven or walked over a high bridge? Perhaps you've thought the higher and longer the bridge, the more substantial should be its guardrails and fences, *especially on a windy day.*

There is a mile-long, 200-foot-high suspension bridge crossing Tacoma Narrows on Puget Sound about 10 miles from our home in the Pacific Northwest. I cross this bridge nearly every day.

Imagine now, you're coming up to that span at 60 miles per hour and you suddenly see there are no guardrails along its sides. The edge of the road is clear and rolls right over a sheer drop into the waters 200 feet below. Will you still cross this bridge at 60 mph? How about if it's a very windy, wet day or it's icy or snowy; are you still at 60?

I suppose some thrill seekers would remain at speed or perhaps even accelerate. I'll speak for myself. I might slow down, find the middle lane, and amble across that bridge in my car at 15 or 20 mph if it's a beautiful, calm day. But I assure you, in any crosswind or snow, I'd stop my car on one side, park it, get out and crawl on hands and knees to the other side where I kept my other car. I'd jump into that car and drive off, later reversing my pattern when I came to that same bridge on the way back home.

Aren't we thankful those guardrails are in place? They allow us to drive faster and safer in all weather conditions than the "sheer drop-off" design. They create for all drivers a predictable path to our destinations, free of the traffic mess caused by the random speeds, bumper-to-bumper conditions and squirrely driving of cars bold enough to negotiate bridges with dangerous, open roadsides.

*Not only do ethics serve as our lighthouses; they serve as our guardrails.*

Our best choices for ourselves and others happen when we navigate dos and don'ts within a predictable pathway bounded by right and wrong. Guardrails aren't iffy or grey or relative; they exist under all driving conditions and are meant to direct all drivers equally. Imagine a set of bridge side rails that were intermittent or could be raised and lowered at the whim of each driver? No, we want our guardrails fixed and shared by all drivers along the entire span of the bridge.

Right choice-making isn't necessarily about sins or illegalities, or laws or philosophical constructs—though these concepts assist us, for sure. Right choice-making happens best on a pathway guided and protected by ethics that are constant and the same for all travelers. Ethics serve as guardrails that allow us to go as fast and as far as we want to go individually, while recognizing collectively that others have the same desire. We should be grateful for these constant guides. They are a privilege, not a penalty.

Let's venture back to that four-way-stop scenario. I don't know about you, but when I stop at that intersection I am not thinking about my state's RCW 46.61.190 (Revised Code of Washington), the law telling me I have to stop before continuing. I'm not thinking about how unethical it would be for me not to stop. I'm probably not even thinking about whether there's a cop hidden somewhere who might ticket me. I stop because I share a trust with you that all of us will stop. The law exists to ensure the trust is reinforced, but it is trust that animates our thinking and our actions at that stop sign.

A four-way stop is a great example of the trust and trustworthiness we need in all levels of society. As on the roadways, where our ability to drive and our quality of life are impacted by our levels of trust, so too, a society of laws without trust doesn't work. We see this in countries all over the world. We've seen glimpses of it here as less-than-accurate stories and false accusations become the mantras of our leadership.

Ethics serve to establish and maintain the trust we need in all of our interactions, including four-way stops. If we are all trusting, then four-way stops work everywhere in the same way. Everyone stops, pauses to take their turn, trusts all others to do the same and then drives on. That's the only way it works all over the globe. Laws don't move us, trust does. **We operate far better on trust without laws than any laws without trust.**

• • • • • • • • • • • • • • • • • • • • • • • • • • • • • • • • • • • •

### INSTANT REPLAY

**Transformation**: a profound change in nature or character

**Universal Morals**: a shared code that supports everyone's common rights

**Universal Ethics**: a shared understanding and practice of what is right and what is wrong through the consistent exercise of human virtues

• • • • • • • • • • • • • • • • • • • • • • • • • • • • • • • • • • • •

## Grace at the Four-way Stop

**The moral**: Whether you believe in a universal moral code or not, the quality of your life is profoundly affected by everyone else who does not.

 **The scenario**: Grace lives in a world of alternative facts, inconsistently practiced virtues and limited universal values. (Sound familiar?)

She believes this is fine because the popular worldview lends itself to her making choices that are best for her. As she pulls up to a four-way stop in her community, she realizes that she may or may not be able to trust others pulling up to that intersection to stop for her. She is painfully aware that some folks follow their own rules, ignore the stop sign and go barreling through the intersection. So, even though she believes she lives in a world where she has more choices, she actually has less. In fact, because there is no trust practiced consistently in her community, she is more profoundly inconvenienced than if she lived in a world where everyone predictably practiced trustworthiness.

Grace begins to realize that, over time, she's not slowing down and waiting for the others she trusts; she has to sit and wait far longer due to the uncertainty of those she mistrusts. To be safe in a world where she has to speculate about other drivers stopping habits, she must wait for everyone to be distant enough from the intersection that she can pass with absolute safety. This means sitting far longer waiting for the road to be clear of all drivers—trustworthy or not! Because in a world without universal principles, who knows?

It turns out where Grace thought she had more freedoms in a place where she can choose her own rights and wrongs, and live by her own ethics, she actually has less choice. The freedom she thought she gained in a world without universal principles is actually far outweighed by the ambiguity of that world where she must guess the ethical from the unethical. The reality is that in a world of universal standards, where trust is consistently practiced, the freedom gained in her ability to trust others far outweighs the faux-freedom of constantly protecting herself from people living by their own ethical standards for their own purposes.

The point of this silliness is that even rule-breakers who want to live by their own changeable ethics and moral standards are affected negatively by all the other rule-breakers. You can only achieve your greatest capacities following agreed-upon moral standards and acting ethically within those standards. Otherwise, at the intersection, you have only two choices: you can stomp on your own personal accelerator to get ahead while you close your eyes to all around you, hoping your luck holds. Or you can be among the trusted, and work to create a world where everyone sees the benefit of that trustworthiness. Universal moral principles provide solid reference points for establishing values, behaviors and ethics that create trust.

## A Universal Code

Whether you want to talk about individuals at a stop sign or a world at the intersection of climate change, increasing economic disparity, resource depletion and socio-political and religious turmoil, I think it's safe to say we all want "trust at the four-way stop" (or in this case, trust at the intersection of 200+ nations).

Ethics are not a relative matter. They are based on the same universally transforming life experiences shared by all of us. These experiences may be interpreted according to our own cultures, ethnicities, life circumstances, family origins, spiritual convictions, etc., but the moral development that results from these transformations is the same. If we circle back to the language codes mentioned in the last chapter, we'll remember that personal codes get us nowhere unless they are shared. The more universally they are shared, the better our ability to communicate truthfully and create trust at a corporate level, family to community to national to international.

So too, we can look at a universal moral code as the lighthouse to a consistent ethic. When we submit to a universal morality that establishes and maintains trust, we don't lose freedoms, we gain them. We practice ethics that make the quality of our lives better because we are assured others are practicing the same ethic to make the quality of their lives better. It is, in essence, our two-fold moral purpose: as we progress morally, so does our community and as our community progresses morally, so too, it impacts on our growth.

> **Ethics Principle No. 5: Being trusted is the foundation of our greatest personal freedoms.**

People can believe we each should create our own codes and follow our own ethical standards—by individual, by group, by nation—but as we saw at the simple four-way stop, the exercise of our virtues is what makes the world go around. Trust is trust is trust, no matter where you are or what you know. It is a universal virtue and its consistent practice animates a world in which we can all achieve our best.

## The Tragedy of Disunity

As I finish writing this chapter, I have a particular sense of sobriety about this topic. Nothing by chance; it was just reported that mass shootings in the U.S. (four or more people killed or injured by gun violence), have increased by 65 percent since 2013. Worldwide, countries with no prior history are experiencing such atrocities. There are undoubtedly more such incidents to come. Of course, our prayers go out to all of those affected by such horrid occurrences.

While the whole truth behind these tragedies is difficult to discern, what we know about such events is that somehow, the people committing the atrocities feel different and apart from their victims. Even those who victimize their own "loved ones" feel separated from their victims.

From an ethics perspective, this separation, this lack of empathy, is a root cause of people disregarding universal moral standards. In this case, standards about the sanctity of life and the right of every human being to practice liberty with responsibility.

There's a lot of voice-raising now over our liberties, as different entities struggle to corral a global pandemic. Individuals and groups focused on individual freedom clash with those who prioritize the long term, community and world health. From an ethical perspective, especially in a crisis, if spread of a virus is accelerated in an environment prioritizing individual freedoms but eradicated from a more effective focus on common moral rights, such as everyone's right to health and safety for all, the latter must take precedence until the problem is wiped out. Seat belt laws, no smoking zones, speed limits, etc., are long standing examples of the right priorities.

An impersonal world full of disunity, divisions, and exclusive, tribal-like "us versus them" mentalities breeds an atmosphere that becomes self-perpetuating. If our ethical choices are defined not by a set of universal moral standards owned by everyone, but by standards individuals or groups apply to themselves willy-nilly, there are no "wrong choices" because all choices by different groups or individuals become "right" for them.

Think of gang members who are willing to steal or maim or kill as part of an initiation ritual to join the group. In this case, their ethic is not based on the universal moral code regarding every soul's right to life or property. Rather, it's based on a gang-authored code that respects only the life of the members—and sometimes, not even that.

Like the four-way stop, our world operates poorly on independent ethical codes. For our greatest individual and collective good—and for progress to be made—our moral standards must be universal.

In a world without universal moral standards, you see acts of violence condoned by perpetrators because of their perceived differences from those they victimize. In their lowest form, such conditions lead to genocide and mass murder. When we do not personalize what we do, then anyone outside our moral circle can be treated the way our standards permit.

This underscores a very important consideration of ethics: **we cannot alone decide on what is ethical and what is not.** Ethics are a public and communal enterprise. This public debate about what is ethical and what is not brings alternative needs into the conversation. In essence, the more public the discussion, the wider the circle. If the circle widens far enough, then "they" become "us." That thought is so frightening for some that they go to unfathomable lengths, including horrid atrocities, to maintain the status quo.

A profound quote from a compendium of talks entitled "The Promulgation of Universal Peace" (1922), seems both timeless and oddly appropriate here, some 100 years later:

> *"It is now the time in the history of the world for us to strive and give impetus to the advancement and development of inner forces—that is to say, we must arise to service in the world of morality, for human morals are in need of readjustment."*

We can more successfully connect and personalize the outcomes of our choices when the stakeholders in our choices have a voice in the results. This is the benefit of universal values: when the "we" includes everyone, there is no longer a "them." I am not suggesting uniformity, but rather unity that respects thriving diversity under the recognition that virtues are universal and should be universally practiced. How do we make this seemingly impossible transition? That's our next subject.

Drive on!

# SHIFT HAPPENS

## *The Threshold of Ethics*

*"Nothing is impossible. The word itself says, I'm possible."*
*—Audrey Hepburn*

A colleague of mine tells an intriguing story about a multi-billion-dollar Canadian pharmaceutical company I'll call pHarmX. Several years ago, pHarmX developed a drug that safely lowers the aldehyde levels of the human body. Now, it's important to bear in mind that humans produce aldehyde after consuming alcohol. It's one of the ways our bodies rid themselves of the alcohol through our breathing. Breathalyzers—those small, portable devices police officers use to test suspected drunk drivers—don't measure alcohol in the breath; they measure exhaled aldehyde. When someone exhales too much aldehyde, it is correlated by this device to excessive alcohol in the bloodstream. Drivers beyond the aldehyde limit—legally drunk—wind up in jail. pHarmX's new, over-the-counter drug had but one purpose: to artificially lower aldehyde levels in human breath, thereby providing false readings on breathalyzers and empowering drunk drivers to avoid arrest, return to their vehicles and head on down the road.

This new drug had passed its tests over several years of research. It was legal. The formula was patented. The drug was highly marketable. And best of all for pHarmX, it was projected by analysts to be a very profitable product. After all, something that helps drunk drivers avoid arrest, courts and expensive tickets has a built-in market of consumers looking to duck responsibility. There was, in fact, already a waiting list for the product. pHarmX was riding high on the possibilities.

Then fate intervened.

With only weeks to go before the new drug's distribution, the teenage daughter of pHarmX's CEO was tragically struck and killed by a drunk driver. This was devastating on its own. But given the company president's support for pHarmX's new drug, it was also remarkably poignant.

My guess is you know what happened to the drug after this accident: pHarmX never shipped it out. In fact, after millions of dollars were spent on research and development, patents, advertising, packaging and distribution contracts, the president of pHarmX scrapped the entire project and destroyed the inventory to ensure the drug stayed out of the marketplace. It was a huge loss to the company. (By the way, he was later fired for this.)

**So, here's the second ethical quandary of this book: As the president of pHarmX, what would you have done about this drug and why?**

What a tremendous emotional impact this awful accident had on this man, his family and the community. Even so, perhaps you're asking yourself, why would any corporate CEO make things worse by throwing away potential profits and scrapping a whole new product line? The answer, of course, lies with ethics! Ethics are interpreted best when they are personalized. When the choice we make has an impact directly on us or on our loved one, it takes on much more potency.

Beyond the incredible challenge of losing his daughter, pHarmX's CEO was visited personally by his company's own ethic—the ethic he had helped create. This tragic accident cut through pHarmX's blind desire to justify profit while risking innocent lives. In fact, it highlighted that those most at risk from pHarmX's new drug weren't its users. It was you and me, the innocent pedestrians and drivers on the same roads as the freed drunkards. It was, in point of fact, this CEO's daughter.

Despite the changes in fortune for the CEO, his family and eventually, his company, the ethical issue in this story was always clear; it just wasn't clearly visible through the clouds of success and profit. The business mandate for "maximizing profit" and the personal goal for "maximizing wealth" became irrelevant after this devastating loss. The CEO's tragedy personalized pHarmX's true objective: to internationally sell a product that covered up potentially deadly behaviors dangerous to all.

In short, the ethical threshold of this CEO was violently breached, and his own moral integrity transformed because of the close personalization of what his company's ethics meant to the quality of others' lives. **This is the most basic expression of good ethics: empathizing with those who have a stake in the results of our actions.**

## Making the Shift: Upgrading Our Ethics

As I outlined in the first chapter, tragedies or sudden challenges in our lives create a shift in what we know and how we feel. This can have a monumental impact on our moral development and accordingly, our ethics. This transformation often moves us from some earlier version of who we were to an upgraded version. I think I'm on Dr. Christopher 23.0 now!

I am reminded of a line from the movie, *The Natural*, where Glenn Close's character comments, "I believe we have two lives: the life we learn with and the life we live with after that." Does it necessarily take a tragedy to make progress? No. But when tragedies happen, we are definitely moved. As for me, I'd rather consciously choose that shift than make it as the result of a tragedy.

Learning and advancing are integral parts of our humanness— we are genetically wired to become more tomorrow than we are today. It's inside our very nature. We develop physically, intellectually, emotionally, and spiritually as we mature. The lesson here is that moral progress and the advance of our ethical capacities are also part of our natural growth.

By way of analogy, consider how babies grow and develop. After the shock of departing the womb's warmth and sustenance, infants (as we all once were) have no recognition of anything beyond their immediate needs. *Feed me. Warm me. Cool me. Hold me. Put me to sleep. Pick me up. Put me down. Change me. Don't change me.* Every newborn infant, everywhere on the globe, for all of history, has started out believing, "This world is ALL ABOUT ME!" (I think I still know some grown-ups with this perspective.) Generally, beyond looks of exploration and imploring innocence, it takes infants weeks, even months, to begin connecting to a world beyond ME.

Eventually, all babies learn to smile. They witness the positive reaction of the children and adults around them with this action, long before there is conscious reasoning. A smile is one of the first witting things a baby can offer beyond itself and it is done for the returned emotional reward. It is social interaction at its most basic level. Perhaps this is why a smile in our later years is so powerful— it has gathered both rational and emotional intelligences that amp up our more instinctual, baby-born potencies.

Consider too, how every infant is tasked to learn a language long before he or she could ever understand the word "tasked." As infants begin to pick up language, through their increased interactions they accomplish something deeper and less immediate than the earlier cries and whoops they mastered.

Fortunately, this learning process doesn't require conscious choice. Rather, we are genetically programmed to learn the languages to which we are exposed by association, assimilation and reinforcement. And babies assimilate Maasai, Mandarin, Japanese, Russian, Swedish, Spanish, French, Tibetan—any language I'd now have a devil of a time learning using only my available intellectual capacities. Babies can assimilate multiple languages at once or even gibberish, if it is consistent enough. They have no choice, just the genetics that provide the capacity.

This genetic ability to advance ourselves is expressed in more ways than the assimilation of smiles and languages. We learn and advance because we have the innate, programmed ability to do so in all aspects of our lives.

If we go beyond these very early, more instinctually-driven years, we can also see the advances though our early education. In fact, our teachers recognized we had latent capacities that could be pushed further as we progressed from grade to grade. Good teachers also knew that whatever we learned had to be governed by our abilities at the time. This is why we are not taught quantum physics in kindergarten. Advances rely on prior knowledge we've mastered. We literally and figuratively require the building blocks first.

## Building Blocks

Consider, if you will, how mathematics was taught to us in grammar school. I don't know about you, but I was taught by my first grade teacher that you could never take a big number from a small number. We learned the concept of numbers by relating them to physical objects. This way we could easily see what they represented. If I only have three blocks on my desk, it's impossible for you to take four of them.

Mathematically speaking, three minus four is impossible, (3-4 = you can't do this!)—it just doesn't make sense at the physical level.

Walt Disney knew well how early learning works and how to explain complex, real-world interactions to his young audience. His studios created nature films that gave animals human characteristics, emotions and even speaking ability. For example, that little otter is mad at his big brother for taking his favorite stick and so swims off in a fret, which unknowingly puts him in danger from that mean old fox downstream. The technical term for this is "anthropomorphizing"—giving human traits to living things to comprehend their behaviors.

Early learning in mathematics is akin to anthropomorphizing animal and plant behaviors. Just as every movement of that little Disney otter is driven by emotions a child understands, so too, every number counts a real object that I can understand: one block, two ponies, three rocketships, etc. As a young learner, this lets me concentrate on the basics of the numbers themselves. I am taught math (and nearly everything else) at my age-bounded capacity for comprehension.

A grade or two later, my capacity is growing, and my teacher is introducing me to negative numbers. This is strange compared to my first grade lessons. Negative numbers aren't real. They don't count actual things—they count what's missing. It turns out, with these conceptual numbers, you *can* take four things away from three things which, with negatives, leaves you a deficit of one thing. We call this deficit "negative one" (-1), which has no tangible representation. Negative one is like a hole. Hmm, maybe negative two is a deeper hole?

Did my first grade teacher lie to me? No, she taught me at my level of comprehension with just enough of a push to nudge my capabilities further along. Having mastered both real and conceptual numbers, in a few years, I'm leaving behind whole numbers and am headed towards fractions, then relating standard numbers with metric numbers, then onward to rationals and irrationals, then to algebraic letters, then geometry, trigonometry, calculus, etc. Our best teachers understand this step-wise learning process of building off one concept to investigate another, always balancing new learning with what we already understand.

Moral standards are learned understandings as well. Our ethical development, like our intellectual and spiritual development, is subject to this same capacity-building process. It is obvious that, as individuals, we live more morally-advanced lives than did people who lived 10,000, 1,000, or even 100 years ago. Can we choose to drink from any water fountain, regardless of our skin color? We couldn't do that in 1960! Can we vote regardless of our gender? Not in 1919! Can we practice any religion we desire? Not in 1635! Can we build public libraries of acquired knowledge? Not in 150 B.E.! Can we take over leadership of the cave-clan by killing off Gronk and his mate? Well, that last one's a stretch, but the rest are cases in point. Morals have progressed even as Gronk steps down from leadership.

Even if there are backwards slips in our progress, we do advance. And whether you want to concern yourself more with our nurturing than our nature, we cannot fight the programming that advances us. We may ignore what we learn. We may buy into a more selfish reality, like an infant. Or we may choose to invest ourselves in a more advanced reality, the furtherance of our rational, emotional and spiritual capacities.

This is where the strong connection to a better ethics conversation lies. Our ability to become more tomorrow than we are today is behind *all* of our personal explorations, transformations, adventures, bold attempts, successes, failures—and our abilities to turn dreams, good or bad, into reality. And as we grow intellectually, emotionally and spiritually (a process referred to at its highest level as self-actualization), our ability to comprehend, practice and advance our morality and our ethical actions follows suit. Self-actualizing then, is both a conscious and unconscious choice.

## What about Good and Evil?

In this light, I offer that the tendency to write off certain actions (or people) as "good" or "evil" is a narrow perspective of our human capacities. Like the simpler lessons of big numbers and little numbers, this worldview was embraced by generations eons back who were bounded by a simpler understanding of the human psyche. Something far more useful now in examining ethical choices is understanding good and evil not as inborn reality, or the temptation of external forces or "bad spirits," but rather as our ability (and personal choice) to live into either our higher nature or our lower nature.

Perhaps, we can even conceive of our lower natures as the past genetic programming and old-world nurturing required for survival in nomadic times before we found the relative protection provided by tribes and villages. Seen in this way, lower nature emotions such as greed, jealousy and covetousness were once important because they ensured our basic survival. After all, in a harsh world, taking, keeping and using—regardless of ownership—often saved our lives.

Yet, today, while these lower-nature emotions are still a part of our genetic heritage, even predominate in some of us, they are ineffective in advancing our collective aspirations and mutual survival. How does jealousy, for instance, advance our mutual progress and moral standards? It cannot. No, jealousy, greed, envy and other self-protective emotions are not positive virtues born of empathy and compassion. They are expressions of fear born of the possessive selfishness that supported our individual survival and helped us win the battles of "we" versus "them" a long time ago.

The four-way stop I mentioned earlier, which operates on the virtue of trust, has the supporting force of law to ensure none of us indulge our selfish desires to run through it. Selfishness doesn't work at a traffic intersection. But selflessness and trust at that intersection empower us to individually and collectively move the fastest, farthest and safest, especially when someone else desires to go a different direction.

I'm not saying good and evil don't exist. I can be "evil" when I live by the dictates of my lower nature—taking care of ME. Evil lives in the withering of virtues caused by my conscious desire to act solely for myself. Good resides in the active demonstration of selflessness and actions that consider the needs of others around me, as well as those of the generations to come.

> *Ethics Principle No. 6: Ethical actions exercise our virtues, the most praiseworthy expression of our higher natures.*

Perhaps another useful analogy is to think of good and evil as a light switch. I can ask you to turn on the light. But I cannot ask you to turn on the dark. Darkness only exists as an absence of light; it is not a reality unto itself. When I extinguish my higher nature, what's left is only the darkness of my lower nature. In this regard then, I would contend that "evil" does not exist except in the absence of good—my higher nature. I believe evil disappears, like the dark, when I turn on the light of more selfless and virtue-driven behaviors.

Can you make good choices believing in the simpler absolutes of good and evil? Yes! If avoiding evil and embracing good leads you to a consistent ethic, then stick with that as your guide. But human behaviors rarely have black and white origins. Viewing our ethical and unethical choices along the continuum of our higher and lower natures provides us a useful tool to examine the complexities of our moral development.

I would compare using the simpler "good and evil" tool in mastering ethics to balancing a checkbook or computing your taxes using Roman Numerals. Imagine: *I got my W-2 for last year showing my total annual income of LVCLXXXI; I spent MLV on gas; I gave MMCCCLXV in cash to charity; subtract XXLIV for mortgage and medical expenses...* oh, it just hurts.

Roman Numeral Tax Form MXL (*that's 1040*)

| | | |
|---|---|---:|
| Income | $ | LVCLXXXI |
| Subtract Expenses | $ | MLV |
| Sub-total | $ | MMCCCLXV |
| Less Mortgage Interest | $ | XXLIV |
| Taxable Income | $ | XLMDCCXXXVI |

*\*Tax Law changes by Congress often feel like Roman Numeral tax accounting*

Add the more advanced Arabic numbers to these processes and suddenly tax reporting takes on higher clarity and greater potency. I suggest it is the same when we use an understanding of our higher and lower natures to empower a new thinking about our ethics. If evil is behind all immoral choices, there is little room for exploring ways to advance ourselves beyond simple edicts such as "stop being 'evil'" or "stop giving in to temptations." This is a bit like the notion that to a hammer, every object is a nail.

We know there are far more tools than hammers and nails needed in construction. The simplistic tendency to label bad choices as the influence of some uncontrollable, external evil takes our own nature away from us. It considerably diminishes the potency of our gift of free will that has the power to choose good over bad and right over wrong.

**Another step toward better ethics, then, is the conscious choice to evaluate where we are along the continuum of our higher and lower natures, leaving behind the simplicity of labeling ourselves and others as "good people" or "evil people."** Our journey towards or away from our higher nature is in our control. Granted, there are factors in our lives, even genetic realities, that may make comprehending and living out of our higher natures difficult. But as humans, we are programmed for growth and advancement. The more power you perceive you have in making good and bad choices, the greater your ability to achieve that growth.

## Commit to the Growth Process

Wittingly or unwittingly, most of us mature from selfish, needy infants to better and more selfless versions of ourselves. As we do, we learn to leave behind small t-truths such as *"the whole world is about me."* Instead, we develop an awareness and understanding of capital T-Truths, such as "I am part of a larger community that only survives through my willing participation in a collective give and take."

Our ability to comprehend our higher and lower natures and our capacity to recognize universal moral principles empower moral progression. This advances not only our physical, emotional and intellectual capacities, but also our spiritual capacities. In fact, I would argue that a component of our development individually and collectively—as a society—is related to an innate (and I would argue spiritual) desire to move our civilization forward. Our answer to the question, "Do we want the quality of our children's lives tomorrow to be better, the same, or worse than the quality of our own lives today?" is a palpable demonstration of our intrinsic need to advance civilization. (By the way, 98 percent of the global audience to which I have posed this question has resoundingly voiced a desire to pass on a better life to future generations.)

When environmental laws were passed in this country in the early 1970s and tree conservation really began to take root (no pun intended), who benefited the most from a more deliberate and careful harvesting of that resource? Not the activists and legislators who enacted it. And not we who have all the wood and paper-based products we desire until our eventual earthly annexation.

For whom were environmental laws passed? It was for the same people for whom we have set aside huge tracts of land in our National Parks. It was for the generations yet to come. It was on behalf of the future stakeholders of trees and other natural resources—most who have yet to be born. It was done for those who cannot yet speak for themselves. This is a very practical example of making ethical choices today that move our society forward tomorrow.

Civilization only exists with a collective of empathetic, cooperating, interdependent people. Bottom line, civilization lasts when people think about more than themselves. The greater our thinking and actions for the betterment of others now and in the future, the more civilized civilization becomes and as history demonstrates, the longer it endures. In that light, our ethical choices on a daily basis come to be far more weighty and impactful.

> *Ethics Principle No. 7: When we take on responsibility for our future generations, it is a selfless act fulfilling our spiritual desire to carry forward an ever-advancing civilization.*

## The Silence Breakers

Sudden tragedies such as ENRON, pHarmX, 9/11, and so many others of our age have the power to shift us from moral auto-pilot to an energized manual control, where we are acutely aware of our actions and their impact. But it doesn't and shouldn't require personal misfortune to switch things up.

It was St. Augustine of Hippo, a bishop in the early third century, who said that hope has two beautiful daughters, anger and courage: anger at the way things are and courage to see that they don't remain that way. Calamities often pique one or both of those emotions, changing our futures so that, at a minimum, such painful lessons are never repeated. The hope of a better world, which comes one person at a time, will require both anger and courage.

In 2017, *Time* magazine announced its Person-of-the-Year: The Silence Breakers. These are the folks who, one person at a time through the Me-Too Movement, have come forward to change an age-old paradigm that there are "weak" people who can be preyed upon for others' personal ends. They have come forward to tear down the cultural acceptance of powerful individuals abusing, harassing and manipulating the "vulnerable." As once-powerful Hollywood moguls, radio and television personalities, corporate executives, government official, religious leaders and others yet to repent are jolted by the capital T-Truths of equality and justice, the costs of their unethical decision-making become crystal clear to everyone. The dominoes are still falling daily.

Never doubt that a rising cry for equity and opportunity can change hearts and grow into a global mind shift. Do the "silence breakers" have special capacities we don't? No, but they do have hope, anger, and courage. Many have also demonstrated unbelievable patience.

Change can take a lifetime or come in the blink of an eye. This is our power individually and collectively. The remainder of this book is devoted to steps in the personal process of creating a better ethic for yourself and, like the silence breakers, changing the world around you one choice at a time.

• • • • • • • • • • • • • • • • • • • • • • • • • • • • • • • • • • • • • •

## INSTANT REPLAY

**Human Capacities**: our ability to do, experience, or understand something and advance from that understanding

**The Continuum of Lower to Higher Nature**: the spectrum of emotions and virtues exercised across a range from fear-driven actions for self toward virtue-driven actions for others

**Self-Actualization**: the self-fulfillment in achieving a potential or talent or in becoming something more today than you were yesterday

**Progressive Morality**: an advance in knowing right or good, based on our ability to move away from our lower natures and toward our higher natures

• • • • • • • • • • • • • • • • • • • • • • • • • • • • • • • • • • • • •

Before we move on to examining how we make this moral shift—and how we progress in our ethical choices, I want to offer one more very important caveat: *don't simply believe me.* Do your own independent investigation of these truths. Try out these ethics suggestions on your own to confirm or deny for yourself what I'm professing. After all, the quality of your life is defined not by the answers you get, but by the questions you ask. Question, question, question . . .

After all, shift happens!

# THE FIRST GRAIN

*The Wisdom of Ethics*

*"Well done is better than well said."*
—*Ben Franklin*

Attempting to condense thousands of years of human advancement in morals, ethics, and philosophy into any one book is akin to holding beach sand in my hands and stating, "Here's what the Washington and Oregon Coasts looks like." It cannot be done.

Or at least, it cannot be done well.

Instead, I'll limit what I'm offering about the why and how of shifting into a higher-nature ethical framework (i.e., living into moral progress) into just four grains from this vast ethics beach. These four vital grains are the result of 20-plus years of intense study and thousands of hours of trainings I've conducted with diverse people and cultures around the globe. Examining these few grains can confirm that your own ethical standards are just fine, or support an advance toward greater consistency, accountability and positive impact in your world. I would argue, they also bring joy in building trustworthiness and respect. Most importantly, these grains are meant to empower your thinking about making consistently better choices in your own life, not just for your own benefit but for the benefit of society both now and tomorrow.

The first grain of wisdom from our ethics beach has much to do with the moral of the pHarmX story. You may recall the shift made by the CEO and his company after his daughter's tragic death and his decision to axe the unethical drug. With a more open mind, he used information and circumstance for personal and organizational transformation.

Let's look at transformation closer to home. I'll bring Grace back into the picture to personalize the difference between having information and using that information for transformative choices.

## The Midnight Swipe

 Grace is driving her moderately-priced vehicle home at 3:00 a.m. one morning through an unfamiliar neighborhood. It's dark and homes are all buttoned up, lights are out and owners are sleeping. As she comes to a corner and turns right, she sideswipes a car parked at the curb. She painfully winces as she hears the two cars scraping together. Without even looking, Grace knows she has done damage to both cars. Since the parked car is one of dozens along the curbside, there's no way to tell which house it belongs to. Besides, it's far too late to go tapping on doors looking for the owner.

Two important questions linger in the air as Grace stops in the road: what should she do? And what does she need to know in order to do it?

Perhaps the answers to these questions are immediate for her. Maybe for Grace, this is a question of treating everyone justly. Leaving a note with her contact and insurance information will do this. So, she already knows everything she needs to know to take the right actions. She immediately stops her car, scribbles a note and leaves it on the damaged car's windshield. She is hopeful the owner will contact her in the morning. Ethics quandary solved! She did the right thing. Off she drives.

Now, since we have access to Grace's thoughts, perhaps she leaves a note, but her hope is that the owner does not contact her—that the wind blows the note away or rain makes it illegible. Or even if readable, perhaps the owner will just let it all go. Grace has still done the right thing, but she has rather selfish thoughts about the outcome. This is a step in the right ethical direction for Grace, although it does leave room for improvement.

For the car owner, Grace's doubts are invisible. The note demonstrates Grace is a good person for doing the honest thing. She has treated this person the way she wants to be treated. Whether the owner contacts Grace or not, she has given him or her the power to decide about the level of care taken with the car. Grace has done right; although her internal motives are a bit shaky, her external actions demonstrate her ethics.

> ### Ethics Principle No. 8: Ethics are in the walking, not the talking!

Let's raise the ethical threshold a notch to see if Grace is challenged to find the right way to do the right thing. We'll add some information that begins to cloud her thinking. If the ethical door jamb is set high enough, she may not cross the moral threshold and do what is right.

Perhaps, the right answer isn't immediate for Grace. So, she slows her car down to think about her options. First option: she could stomp on the accelerator and speed off into the night, rationalizing that there's really no harm here—a few scratches on a dumb old car and no one was hurt. She already has to pay for her own car repair anyway.

Second option: Grace needs more information before taking any action. She begins to tackle the issues one at a time.

1.  Maybe she should know the make, model and age of the car first? Will this help her choice? Probably not. It seems irrelevant, unless Grace wants to rationalize fleeing the scene to avoid trouble she somehow associates with this type of car. Or she thinks this car is an ugly, unpopular model. My guess is, if she was going to leave a note or vamoose, the choice has very little to do with the model and manufacturing date of the car.

2.  Maybe it's more about the condition of the car rather than its age? What if the car looks abandoned? What if it's covered with mud, bird droppings and leaves? Maybe this should stop her from leaving the note? It's sure useful information to rationalize speeding away, but again it seems of no use in deciding the right thing to do.

3.  What if the car has no tabs and no license plates? It's definitely abandoned! Does she need information about whether or not striking an abandoned car is illegal before she leaves the note? No, her lack of understanding of the law is no excuse anyway. And what does the law have to do with doing the right thing in this case? [By the way, a Washington State Trooper in one of my trainings once told us it is illegal in this State to strike any vehicle and leave the scene without identifying yourself.] Again, this is an interesting tidbit, but even if Grace knows this information, how is it useful in deciding whether to do the right thing?

4.  What if, as she gets out of her car, she notices the damaged car is parked illegally—it's too close to the corner and too far away from the curb. In fact, it's pretty evident that's why she scraped it. Should this information impact her decision?

5.  Does Grace need to know the clauses and restrictions in her own insurance policy before deciding to do the right thing? For instance, whether her policy covers hitting parked or abandoned vehicles? What about her deductible?

Hmmm, I can see Grace beginning to hesitate as the threshold gets higher... her foot is getting really itchy over that accelerator!

6. Let's make this worse. What if Grace just recently had an accident and her insurance company warned her that another accident this year will either cause her rates to sky-rocket or her coverage to be dropped? Should this factor into her thinking about that note?

Uh-oh, Grace is locking her door again and her car is beginning to inch forward. Let's ask her a few more questions.

7. Let's say this old car she sideswiped is properly licensed, but there are already so many dings, dents, and scrapes on it, Grace cannot tell whether she even hit it. Does she need to see the damage she caused to the car before she decides to leave the note? (The damage on Grace's car and the scraping metallic sound ought to be proof enough, but she wants to see the damage she caused. And if she does leave this scraped-up old car behind without a note, what difference will one more scrape make anyway?) But should she decide for the owner what is or isn't visible to him or her?
8. There's another piece of information that might be useful. Does Grace need to know who owns the car before she leaves a note? If the car is in such bad shape, it's probably owned by someone who doesn't care, right? And even if they do care it seems like they can't afford to go after her legally anyway. It seems safe to take off before being caught.
9. But what about the opposite scenario? What if the car Grace sideswiped is an expensive, well-cared for luxury vehicle? I guess Grace can go two ways on this one. Either this expensive car is owned by someone who can take care of the damage themselves or this luxury car means the owner

*can* afford to really come after her. Perhaps the car is even owned by a lawyer???

Should any of this additional knowledge matter to Grace when choosing to do the right thing?

I don't know if any of these scenarios raised your ethical threshold to the point you're urging Grace to drive away. I do know that we can often look for information or knowledge that helps us rationalize making a wrong choice.

If we follow the Golden Rule consistently and treat others the way we want to be treated, none of the answers to these questions matter in making the ethical decision. Grace should leave the note in hopes the owner will contact her so he or she can be made whole. That is what Grace would want if someone hit her car in the middle of the night. Anything else is Grace's struggle to try and find a right way to do the *wrong* thing.

## Bringing It Closer to Home

I bet many of you have parked your car in a store lot, gone off to shop and come back to find some scratch or dent in your car door along with no note. Did you wish the perpetrator had identified his or her responsibility to you to at least help pay for the repair? I have!

No, the right thing for Grace to do was clear from the beginning. All the additional information in the world will make it no clearer. In fact, it makes it greyer.

With one last question, perhaps we can get Grace to stop again and leave a note. Let's say she thought about all of the excuses we covered, but she knows or is related to the parked cars owner. We will personalize the victim of the sideswipe for her.

Instead of a stranger, what if Grace knows she has damaged her best friend's car? Or her brother's car? Or her mother's car? (Oh, with that last one, she's definitely driving away again . . .)

Did these facts make a difference to the speed of Grace's answers? Should they make a difference—treat a known person more justly than an unknown one? Is this the derivation of the Golden Rule: do unto others *you know* as all others should do unto you? If so, then perhaps the issue became more about ethics and less about Grace the closer the situation got to impacting her own family or friends. As I've stated before, more equity happens when our right and wrong outcomes are personalized.

> ***Ethics Principle No. 9: Ethics are best understood when they are personalized.***

The ability to practice "right" when it involves those we know and "wrong" against those we don't means our ethics only protect those we already care for. If that's true, no stranger should ever do a good deed for us either. So much for the Good Samaritan, or donating to non-profits, or being of service to others, or asking for directions from a stranger, or borrowing sugar from your new neighbor and so on. This can't be the equitable, compassionate and just world we want to live in, can it?

Ethics are practiced universally. We should gauge our decisions on the outcomes for all those impacted now or in the future. This is one component of the shift toward ethical transformation. We don't raise and lower our ethical thresholds to do right to those we care about and wrong to others. **Ethics tell us the right and wrong actions toward everyone.** It doesn't matter what or who we know; that is knowledge. The only thing that matters in our shift toward selflessness and moral progression is understanding that everyone, known and unknown, is owed the right action.

## The Difference between Knowledge and Wisdom

At the heart of this shift is understanding the difference between knowledge and wisdom. Knowledge is not wisdom; how you use your knowledge is an indicator of your wisdom. And the bridge between your knowledge and your wisdom is ethics.

> *Ethical Principle No. 10: Knowledge is not wisdom; how you use your knowledge is an indicator of your wisdom. And what bridges the gap between your knowledge and your wisdom are your ethics.*

In the case of Grace's sideswipe, the answers to all her questions weren't leading her to make the right choice. In fact, as we watched Grace, some of her answers were used to rationalize the wrong choice. Wisdom is making the right choice, sometimes despite the knowledge you have. Our ethics are the bridge between what we might know and what we should do about it.

Let me provide another true example that breaks wisdom into three requisite pillars. After 9/11, I was asked to speak in numerous venues about the morality of the tragedy. The hijackers had obviously believed they were doing the right thing, just as any "soldier" at war can. I was asked many times if, given their strong convictions, the hijacker's decisions were moral for them. In other words, if they felt so strongly they were making the right choice in using planes and passengers as weapons of terror, were they really wrong? There are two perspectives we must bring to bear in a moral answer to this question.

First of all, the question itself legitimizes the perspective that what's moral can change from time to time and place to place. If this is so, then I often offer in response, do we want a morality so flexible that all actions are moral if an individual or group or nation believes in them strongly enough? Isn't this what drove the Holocaust during World War II? How about a nation or group's strong convictions to allow bribery, slavery or child labor? What about a belief in isolating the mentally ill or senile?

Aren't we starved for a universal morality where everyone's common rights are respected? The moral answer is we should be. Did the 9/11 terrorists weigh these common rights? No, they used the moral code of their "guild" (their association or sphere of influence) to disregard universal rights and practice their own beliefs on unwitting others. Such practices, once rationalized by the chosen few, become a tool to divide in conviction and in fact.

The second perspective on morality relies on an understanding of wisdom's three pillars: our rational intelligence (knowing the right thing to do), our emotional intelligence (feeling right about what we do) and our spiritual intelligence (actually doing right, because of or despite what we know or how we feel).

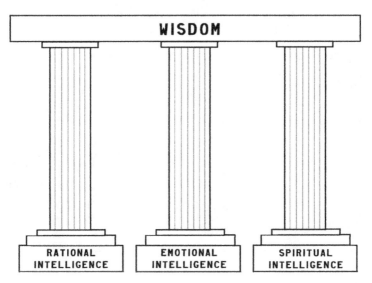

THE THREE PILLARS OF WISDOM

The terrorists who committed the 9/11 atrocities certainly had rational intelligence, the first pillar of wisdom. They were smart enough to learn from simple training how to pilot complex aircraft into specific targets. They had no flying experience. I got my pilot's license in 1980 and it can still be tricky to land a small plane on a big runway at 80 miles per hour in a big crosswind. Imagine the complexity of piloting a passenger jet at 600 miles per hour into a target just as wide as its wings. In a very unfortunate way, they demonstrated they had intellectual capacity.

What about emotional intelligence, the second pillar of wisdom? What do the terrorists' feelings mean to the wisdom of what they did? They were willing to give their lives to complete their task. That's the most significant emotional investment any of us can make. If I were asked, "Are you willing to give your life for something?" I'd have to think long and hard about my answer. I hope, given no other choice, I would sacrifice myself to save my daughters, my wife or someone in desperate peril but I won't really know this until it happens, God forbid. These folks demonstrated profound emotional intelligence in giving their lives to save others within their circle. In another unfortunate way, they demonstrated the strength of their emotional capacity.

What about spiritual intelligence, the third pillar? I do not mean their commitment to certain religious tenants, rightly or wrongly interpreted. I mean, did they demonstrate care for others outside of their brethren, their families, friends and countrymen? Did they consult with everyone whose lives would be impacted by their actions before they made their choice? The people outside of their circle were still stakeholders in their choices—the folks who had a stake in the outcome of their actions. It would be one thing for the nearly 3000 people who died in the collapsing towers to have agreed to give their lives this way for this cause. It is another ethical matter entirely to be innocently sacrificed.

And beyond the stakeholders who gave their lives were the stakeholders who were permanently or temporarily injured physically or emotionally by the terrorists' actions. These included first responders, families, friends, neighbors, surviving co-workers and those who share the moral conviction about everyone having a right to life, safety and security. In this case, that's a huge number of stakeholders—perhaps hundreds of millions or billions around the world.

Given the horrendous cost of the hijacker's actions, their effect is so cataclysmic and widespread, it is a virtually impossible ethical duty to consult with all the stakeholders before this action is taken. Silly, yes. But impact on others is impact on others, no matter how few or how many. And in-point-of-fact, the terrorists intended the shock, surprise and horror that occurred that day for all global stakeholders anyway. They knew the level of attention this atrocity would bring their cause. Horror is part of that weapon.

A demonstration of spiritual intelligence, the third pillar of wisdom, would have encompassed an understanding of those potentially affected, especially those stakeholders bound with making the ultimate sacrifice. No, the terrorists' actions were arbitrary, unilateral and done for the benefit of just a few—those they cared about. The acid test of their spiritual double-standard would be carrying out the same deadly actions if they discovered family members or close friends were housed in the exploding towers or on board the weaponized aircraft. Under those conditions, it seems clear given their history their choice would be different. If so, in the tragedy of 9/11, they were treating some more equally than others and that is not an action of spiritual intelligence.

With this significant pillar missing, one can judge the action immoral because it lacked wisdom. And there's the answer to the question: were they moral or not in the conviction of their beliefs? Vengeance, mercilessness and perseverance are potent weapons, but impotent morally. These are lower nature emotions devoid of love and based upon fear. Do actions based on those foundations sound ethical?

. . . . . . . . . . . . . . . . . . . . . . . . . . . . . . . . . . . .

## INSTANT REPLAY

**Knowledge**: facts, information and skills acquired by a person through experience or education

**Wisdom**: the integration of knowledge, experience and a deepened understanding that is embodied by the sum of our rational, emotional and spiritual intelligences

**Stakeholders**: those who are affected by a course of action; having a stake in the outcomes

. . . . . . . . . . . . . . . . . . . . . . . . . . . . . . . . . . . .

Bottom line: no matter how much you know or how strongly you feel about what you know, you must go beyond the small group around you and involve others, especially the stakeholders, in a determination of your morality. The less we involve others, the more ethical we feel about our choices.

## The Powers of Empathy and Compassion

The classic tale of the Good Samaritan illustrates how the powers of empathy and compassion serve to drive mutually beneficial relationships. The story of a man who risks himself on a dangerous road to help another poor, unfortunate traveler, left beaten and robbed, is not a story of sainthood or piety. Rather, it is a parable about the human capacity to develop and demonstrate the three pillars of wisdom. The story urges us, like the Good Samaritan, to step beyond our own concerns and into the shoes of others, even our enemies, in order to understand their concerns.

What's the difference between the man who stopped to help and the others who passed the victim by? It is the framing of the questions they asked themselves. To the selfish, the important question is, "If I stop to help this man, what will happen to me?" To the empathetic and selfless, the important question is, "If I don't stop to help this man, what will happen to *him*?" In the second question—and its answer—are evidenced all three pillars of wisdom: our rational, emotional and spiritual intelligences.

This adds poignancy to the concept that the quality of our lives is not measured in the answers we find, but in the questions we ask. The next chapter provides some profound opportunities to shift the questions we ask about morality and ethics.

# THE SECOND GRAIN

*The Whole Truth of Ethics*

*"I'll see it when I believe it!"*
*—Joel Barker*

The heart of moral progress can be appropriately seen as a "paradigm shift." In this case, the paradigm shift toward a more advanced understanding of morality and ethics has three fundamental sources:

1. It is a function of our conscious choice.

2. It is part of our genetic programming.

3. It depends on habitual behaviors—that is, living with a habit of repeatedly making good choices and witnessing their outcomes.

The word paradigms (pronounced like "pair-a-dimes," although that's not 20 cents, some jokingly point out) comes from the Greek word, *paradeigma*, meaning model or pattern. In this case, it is the model or pattern of our truths.

We use paradigms to interpret and understand the world around us. The old 'flat earth' paradigm fit the pattern we saw as we walked the land. That pattern didn't fit well the land sinking below the horizon as we sailed far from shore. So, we eventually changed the paradigm— land disappears below the horizon, therefore the world must be curved. Even round?

We look for patterns to make sense of things. And we create those patterns with our truths. If a pattern we rely on does not fit what we are observing, we have two choices: we can change the pattern to help us make sense of the new reality or we can modify the new reality to fit the old pattern. The latter is easier to accomplish because paradigms (our truths) are powerful and not so easily changed. But the reward and true reality appear in shifting our paradigms to fully discover a new truth.

Perhaps a few examples would help to clarify this weighty concept.

## Ah, Spit!

 Let's bring Grace into the scenario. Grace shares a paradigm so strongly with the rest of us that it seems nearly instinctual: the capital T-Truth that everyone is born with the right to live in freedom. Our forefathers emigrated here with that belief. It was discussed and refined by our nation's founders in creating the Declaration of Independence, the Constitution and the Bill of Rights. These and more are laws were premised on our paradigms about freedom. We have gone to war, even within our own country, to empower those freedoms as every person's inalienable right.

From a moral perspective, this paradigm ensures fundamental standards that encompass independence, equity, equality and so much more. It is a capital T-Truth so basic in this guild (the United States), we don't need to debate its truth; we simply and clearly know it is true and we live our lives on the basis of that truth.

Grace is nodding her head rambunctiously.

When we bump up against nations or cultures that don't operate with this truth, say a communist system of governance, we fight intellectually, emotionally, physically and even spiritually to bring the non-believers into the capital T-paradigms on freedom and independence.

We can also see what happens when the small t-paradigms create patterns that don't fit our reality. Again, we are pushed to make changes either to the pattern or to the things that don't fit it.

A quick example. Despite the fact our Founding Fathers were creating revolutionary documents declaring people's inalienable rights, some of them willfully owned slaves. How could this behavior fit the capital T-paradigm about freedom for all? Well, as I said, one way to ensure a paradigm remains intact is to change the world to fit the erroneous paradigm. In this case, people who are owed freedom should get it and the rest aren't really people. This small t-truth allows free people to own non-people. The non-people don't deserve the freedoms of the guild. Therefore, our founders argued for total independence for *all people* while owning what were to them, *non-people*.

That small t-truth, that non-people exist and can be owned, was such an error in our founding that we would go to war just 80 years later—with Americans killing nearly three-quarters of a million of other Americans—to prove this paradigm had to change. In the end, it did, mostly. After four-plus bloody years of civil war, we would begin to apply the capital T-Truth, the universal paradigm bereft of conceiving of anyone as a non-person. After this, we started the slow journey toward enforcing everyone's rights to join the guild called humanity and enjoy every freedom afforded by it. This shift is so difficult for some, we still have civil demonstrations to advance the same rights for all.

The difficulty with paradigms is that we don't always recognize which are "small t" and changeable and which are "capital T" and should remain unchangeable. This is especially true for the paradigms we believe so deeply we rarely discuss them.

Not seeing which truths should change and which are universal can be a problem, especially when it comes to applying these truths in moral situations. We can believe in some paradigms so strongly that whether they are small t-truth or capital T-Truth is irrelevant to us. We know the truth is the Truth.

Perhaps we can personalize the concept of paradigm shifts and small t- and capital T-Truths by using a slightly provocative example. This may feel a bit frivolous, yet it emphasizes how deeply we imbed paradigms even when they are more perception than reality. Okay, first, let me ask Grace about this strong paradigm we all share. Although I don't know where we learned it, most all of us know it as truth.

Let's pretend I ask a group of the folks reading this book to come to a presentation on ethics. As they enter the room they are each given a small paper cup. They sit down, cup in hand and once I'm up on stage, I ask everyone to spit into their cup. (Uh-oh, Grace is already squirming.)

If that particular request isn't gross enough, to the audience's shock, I ask them a moment later to put the cup back to their lips and drink. (Wow, Grace is leaving the room. Wait, hang on, there is a good point to be made here . . .).

If you can look past the provocative nature of this less-than-Miss Manners example, there is a strong paradigm here we all share even though it has no basis in reality. If you've been grossed out already like Grace, your reaction is actually an expression of how deeply this paradigm can run in us. "Yuk" is a strong, emotional reaction to someone pushing against our truth and this is a truth so strong we aren't even supposed to discuss it in polite company. Spit has an important meaning, doesn't it? In some cultures, it's very symbolic.

Go ahead, I can feel the angst growing in the room, "YOU DON'T SPIT IN FRONT OF A GROUP OF STRANGERS AND YOU DEFINITELY DON'T EVER RETURN IT TO ITS PLACE OF ORIGIN!"

Let me ask Grace, "How do you know these rules about spitting?" Grace says she got them from her parents. I think I did too, although I don't remember any specific lessons about my saliva. As a baby, I could drool all over the place. Perhaps this spitting thing is similar to the advances my teething or my toilet training would bring?

Somehow, we seem to have inculcated this paradigm from those around us.

Spit *is* gross, isn't it? We just know it, somehow. It feels almost instinctual—although it's not. Even worse, is the concept of re-using it. That's an even stronger truth. Did anyone teach you that stronger truth, or did you just know that somehow?

Grace is squeamishly admitting she just picked that part up herself, especially since she is a lady. This truth then seems to have a gender bias. Social pressure about spitting must not be gender neutral in this culture. After all, the baseball men spit in stadiums full of tens of thousands of fans and it's beamed on television to millions worldwide. Grace is nodding emphatically.

Somehow, we all know the capital T-Truth about spit. We do not necessarily know how we know it. And we seem to know it so well, we ought not to talk about it much. So, Grace is asking, "Why are you talking about it? Show some couth, for crying out loud!"

Just a few more silly questions. Is there any difference between what's in that cup and what's in your mouth right this second? Biologically? Chemically? Socially? Anything?

"No?"

So, spit inside the mouth, okay. Spit inside the cup, questionable at best! Maybe we could say there are some social standards that the stuff in the cup violates, but again, there's nothing harmful physically.

"Is it okay to share spit with others?"

"NO!", Grace is saying as she stands up to leave again. "What about when we kiss one another?" I boldly ask. "That's different," she's exhorting.

"How is it different?" I ask.

"Well," she offers, "It's fine, even pleasant, but no one thinks about it that way!"

"So, the gross is in the perspective, not in the truth. If we look at the same act differently, kissing or on the sports field, it ceases to be so gross?" I posit.

Grace is getting very quiet.

I want to ask, "How about the cup thing with another person? Can that be offered to someone you care about?"

Grace is mumbling something about the Marquis de Sade and shaking her head. Our shared paradigm about spit makes you ponder, doesn't it?

Okay, let's leave the graphic descriptions and gross behaviors behind and consider the use of this "example" as a small t-truth that feels strongly like a capital T-Truth.

I would offer, by the way, that faced with dehydration or death and no other alternatives, because there is no biological reason to avoid it, any of us might think about drinking most anything—gross be darned—in favor of survival. It has been done. So too, there are a host of semi-polite ways spit is used in our society. Our mothers dabbed dirt off our faces with a little on a napkin or shirt sleeve. We often use a bit of spit to wipe a food or dirt stain off our bare skin, or a good blouse. We're even allowed to use it for helping a loved one. But while it's okay to dab some from your tongue onto a towel or Kleenex or napkin for cleaning purposes, it's not okay to spit directly onto the stain and then use the towel to wipe it off. No, we all know the Truth is that the transport method for "clean-up" spit is important too. Again, I don't know how we know this strong paradigm, but we do. And again, it's so strong, I keep having to apologize for this impolite example. In fact, I take it all back!

The paradigm in this case is in our heads, not in anything physical, and it is small t-truth because it can change, dependent upon our circumstances. We may feel very strongly about this paradigm, but it's not based on rational intelligence, or even physical truth; it's somehow a part of our emotional intelligence. That's one of the reasons this truth can change.

As we examine moral standards in our cultures, it is important to keep this concept in mind. A strong belief can be strong enough to make us see it as capital T-Truth. But a strong belief does not make it so. As we begin to look at the historic ways we've examined and understood our morality and our ethical actions in the past, it may be important to wittingly examine what we know is truth and keep a keen eye on what is or is not the capital T variety.

## My Two Cents on Paradigms

Changing a paradigm is one of the most significant transformations we make in our lives. We believe in our paradigms so strongly, we even turn unjust, small t-truths into unjust laws. Segregated drinking fountains (and bathrooms and restaurants and schools, etc.), no vote for women, unfair labor practices and so on are examples of past paradigms that needed an infusion of pure, capital T-Truth. Unfortunately, some of that infusion is still seeping in too slowly.

Some hold on to small t-truths about racism, sexism, ageism, etc., essentially using them to withhold vital rights for millennia, and swearing to their immutability. We slowly make moral advances and we eventually replace them with capital T-Truths. This change comes in our habits our laws. Concepts such as desegregation, gender equity, equal access and livable wages, that once withered, now flourish in a capital T environment. Don't get me wrong, we may still have some distance to go, but individually and collectively we have advanced well past the creation and enforcement of most unjust laws.

By the way, in his work on paradigms, author Joel Barker discovered two very interesting things about paradigm shifts:

1. Every paradigm shift goes through three phases: *Ridicule, Persecution,* and *Acceptance.* The *Ridicule* stage occurs as a truth begins to shift and the owners of that old truth look down on the initial

few who believe in the different and eventually more potent truth. "Oh, aren't those Round-Worlders a crazy bunch here in our flat world." The *Persecution* stage happens as the ranks of the new-truth believers swell and the old-truth believers who gained power and influence under the old belief become threatened. After all, if the truth shifts, the power-holders might lose what they have! "Hey, we gotta do something; there are so many of these Round-Worlders popping up, everyone's gonna wind up falling off the edge! They have to be stopped before everyone believes this craziness, people get hurt, and we upset our flat-world empire!" The *Mass Acceptance* stage comes when the new-truth believers strategically outnumber the old-truth believers. In fact, the tirades and oppression growing through the *Persecution* stage serve to advertise the new truth more widely. Almost overnight, non-believers accept the new truth as if they always believed it, even claiming at times, they started it. "A round world? Of course, it is! I'm the first to have sent my trade ships farther out to sea! Their discoveries have been great for all of us and rebuilt this empire!"

Galileo's crazy truth about Earth not being at the center of the universe was first seen as scientific incompetency *(Ridicule)*. But it was also dangerous to the Church's doctrine placing man at the center of God's creation. So, the Church arrested Galileo and his followers and forbade the teaching of this heresy *(Persecution)*. That didn't work when countless other scientists and theologians began to prove Galileo was right. So, the sun-centered model of the universe continued its spread and the earth-centered model shrank away. Faced with 200 years of overwhelming opposition, the Church not only relented and decreed Galileo's model the new capital T-Truth, but mandated everyone to believe it *(Mass Acceptance)*. While every paradigm shift goes through some version of these three stages, the strongest beliefs may take centuries or longer to complete the transition.

Some shifts *are* completed in what seems the blink of the eye. This is rare and often catalyzed by a crisis or tragedy. For instance, people today describe how their world changed when they lost a loved one, or after an accident, or when a diagnosis was shocking or when world events leapt out at them. How many people who witnessed 9/11 can remember where they were and what they were doing at that moment? This horrific injustice changed our perception of the world. The problems of the Middle East were once just three-minute sound bites on CNN or NBC. After 9/11, we see the injustices in the Middle East and other parts of the world with a bit more empathy. Our role in world affairs gains a responsibility we did not perceive on 9/10. A similar attack in history, Pearl Harbor, caused a parallel shift nearly overnight. We left the paradigm (small t-truths) of isolationism behind to enter World War II. Before 1941, the Nazis invading Paris was, to us, a ho-hum event in European affairs. Now it's impossible to imagine such an unreal perception of our global responsibilities despite changing administrations.

> ## *Ethics Principle No. 11: With paradigms, a truer truth always wins!*

2. The second thing Barker noted about paradigm shifts has to do with the roles we play in the shifting. In every paradigm shift there are *Scouts, Pioneers*, and *Settlers. Scouts* go out looking for a new truth when the old one becomes impotent in answering new questions. *Pioneers* follow the *Scouts* on the trails they blazed and become the first to take advantage of the benefits of the new truth. They also show the rest of us those advantages. Lastly, *Settlers* follow the *Pioneers* and leverage as much out of the new truth as possible.

Galileo was a scout. Educators, students, and scientists of the time were pioneers. The Church and rest of the world became settlers.

## Change the Menu!

During my thesis research in the mid-2000s, it became clear I was going to have to be a paradigm *Scout*. As more and more high-profile cases such as ENRON, Arthur Anderson, TYCHO, WorldCom, Madoff, Countrywide, the 2008 financial crisis and more appeared in the news, questions arose in my classrooms and consulting venues. We needed a more effective conversation about our ethics. The old one obviously wasn't working.

These "older" scandals have been replaced by newer ones. We talk today about Volkswagen, Boeing, Theranos, Wirecard, the Opioid crisis, foreign election interference and so on. Same old wine, brand new, slightly chipped bottles.

Since the originators of these ethical gaffs believe themselves to be highly moral people, our paradigms about ethical decision-making need re-assessment. I wrestled mightily with how the traditional moral philosophies and our ethical frameworks were not as potent as they once had been—a round world waiting for the new paradigm to better recognize it. A world trending away from the sanctity of tribes and states and nations and toward a global community, even a new global sovereignty, has raised significant questions about moral standards and ethical choices that the old frameworks frankly can't answer. In fact, faced with the greatest diversity of cultural, ethnic and gender influences, educational backgrounds and individual perceptions seated at the growing global table, the old truths are woefully inadequate to answer our emerging needs concerning right and wrong choices.

How should one country half-a-world away from another respond to environmental travesties that affect the whole world? How should a limited resource that is being over-exploited by one or a few nations be preserved for all? Who polices the promises, agreements, laws and rights that emerge among the global guild? Who organizes the groups that will enforce our promises to one another? Is it time for a global currency to end the horrid waste of international exchange rates? (Can you imagine if every state of our Union still had its own currency?)

In a free market world, how do we detour the waste from underpriced goods that squeeze companies into and out of existence? What can be done to curb the by-products of overconsumption? How do we reconcile the disparity between parts of the world faced with an obesity epidemic while other parts are faced with starvation? This is only a fraction of the new questions forcing a new moral paradigm.

While these appear to be political or economically driven, at their heart are large, ethical concerns about the recognition and enforcement of universal moral principles modeled on the capital T-Truths of equity and equality, socio-economic justice, global rights and much more.

• • • • • • • • • • • • • • • • • • • • • • • • • • • • • • • • • • • • •

## INSTANT REPLAY

**Paradigm**: fundamental rules or truths that define our boundaries as well as how to act or behave within those boundaries

**Paradigm Shift**: the change to a new set of fundamental rules or truths that often changes our perspectives on the reality of the world

**Three stages of a paradigm shift**:
*Ridicule*: mocking, deriding or belittling those who follow a new truth
*Persecution*: oppressing, victimizing or otherwise abusing the new believers
*Mass acceptance*: the shift in majority agreement or belief in the new truth

**Scouts**: the free-thinkers who seek a new paradigm when the old one ceases to effectively answer the latest problems

**Pioneers**: the first people who take actions based on the new paradigm

**Settlers**: the majority of people who, following the pioneers, take full advantage of the new paradigm

• • • • • • • • • • • • • • • • • • • • • • • • • • • • • • • • • • • •

We need an infusion of Truth into our decision-making. I am not suggesting this is about throwing good systems away and starting everything over. This is about reframing the way we meet ethical challenges so we are always recognizing universal principles and stakeholder rights.

Let me use one last example that may be a bit surprising. Let's look at McDonald's.

McDonald's represents a world-encompassing food supply and distribution chain based on the cutting edge of food science. Think about it. From the flavors, seasonings, combinations and presentations of the food, to the colors and textures in the restaurant, to the elements that make up the tables and counters, to the freezing, cooling, keep-warm and cooking equipment, to the drive-through packaging and convenience, these factors and others are outcomes of modern food science.

McDonald's is literally a global marvel of our food chain. You can walk into any one of thousands of outlets located in nearly every corner of the world and in four minutes or less, get exactly the same food made of the same ingredients in the same proportions with the same consistency and flavor at the same temperature in the same packaging for nearly the same price. And in some places, that's all available 24/7. Nothing like this existed, even in the military, just 40 or 50 years ago. In fact, with all of this successful technology and food science knowledge, there is only one thing glaringly wrong with McDonald's— THE MENU!

Imagine using this same technology and the massive food supply and distribution chains at McDonald's command to serve nutritious food around the earth. Imagine if McDonald's, acting as an agent of change, took on the task of serving every child on the planet at least one hot, healthy meal per day, every day of the week, 365 days per year? Change the menu and McDonald's becomes one of the greatest forces of socio-economic justice the world has ever seen. (By the way, the Clinton administration actually started an initiative to feed every child on the planet one nutritious meal per day. I bet we could raise that to three meals if we really tried.)

I'm not suggesting McDonald's has to become a subsidized, non-profit organization to do this. They have their own profitable mission and should live into it. I am suggesting that without changing any of their infrastructure, their systems or their technology, they can feed the world. Given the obesity epidemic in this country, there's another useful benefit to a healthy, global diet.

We can think about our modern systems of democracy, capitalism, spiritualism and others in the same way. A change of moral thinking isn't about revolution. These systems don't need to be scrapped, what's on their current menus does. With the right motives and morals, these systems will serve a world of universal principles and just laws exceedingly well.

So, how do we keep the systems and change what's on their menus? We need a paradigm shift regarding the small t- and capital T-Truths of our ethics. We don't have to overthrow thousands of years of moral debate. We need to use that strong heritage and shift our thinking about how we make good choices and give up bad choices. But before we jump to that shift, it is important we review how we got ourselves into all this.

# THE THIRD GRAIN

*The Philosopher's Versus the Practitioner's Ethics*

*"Truth is a single point which ignorant men have multiplied."*
*—Muhammad*

We can't tell the whole story of ethics without at least glancing at the classic moral frameworks we use to justify our behaviors. These generally have titles ending in the suffix "ism." This is just a fancy way to turn anything into a practice or philosophy, like activism or Buddhism or that famous tongue twister, antidisestablishmentarianism. You can add Ism to nearly any noun and it becomes an active practice or a learning. I'm not sure there's a mountainism or oceanism or an ice creamism, but there should be. You could say, by reading this book you are learning Graceisms or Dr. Gilbertisms. Or not.

All this to say, don't be impressed or confused by the upcoming Isms. Concentrate on their root word. For example, Consequentialism is the practice of ethics based on the consequences of a choice in order to determine its morality.

It is also vital to understand two things up front as we dive into these frameworks.

Firstly, as I've noted earlier, it is very rare that anyone making an unethical choice looks at it as unethical. Instead, we use these frameworks to rationalize our choices and to see them as ethical, even defendable to others, if just in the short term.

Secondly, we seldom examine or even know which ethical framework we're using in our decisions. For example, imagine, before cutting someone off on the freeway or making an illegal copy of a DVD, thinking to yourself, "Well, am I going to use Relativism or Consequentialism today to justify this?" It obviously doesn't happen that way. We choose an action and then we act. We usually rationalize that action before, during and afterwards, utilizing many excuses. These self-justifications fall into five general perspectives or frameworks that social scientists, philosophers and ethicists describe with these Isms.

Thirdly, despite the appearance that "philosophical ethics" are abstract and far removed from applications to our lives, these frameworks interpret and label the ways we consciously and unconsciously organize our thoughts to answer our ethical conundrums.

Before we familiarize ourselves with the five major ethical frameworks in the next chapters, let me provide a quick example of a few of them in practice. It's important to remember that these frameworks can actually muddle the issues. They can be contradictive, exclusionary, paradoxical and often downright confusing in our understanding of what is right and what is wrong.

Speaking of confused, let's get Grace back in the room.

## Grace's Twenty-Dollar Quandary

**The moral**: No matter how you justify a good choice or a poor one, your rationalizations generally fall into one or more of the traditional ethical frameworks—the Isms.

 **The scenario**: Grace has gone shopping and at the check-out stand she hands the clerk a $100 bill for her groceries. He gives her change and she walks out with her bagged goods. When she gets home, she sees the clerk handed her $20 more in change than she was owed. What should she do and why should she do it? Grace doesn't have an immediate answer. She needs to think about this one. The ethical response would be to take the $20 back right away or at least the next time she returns to that store.

Without realizing it, she starts to rationalize a few things. At first, she thinks, "Well, no one knows about this, so I can't get into trouble. Maybe I can keep this $20?" The ethical framework she's using unwittingly to feel fine about keeping the $20 is called *Subjectivism*. She's looking at this choice from the *subjective* perspective— thinking only about what happens to her. Keeping the money is a great outcome for her. If she thinks she might get into trouble for keeping the $20, and she decides to take it back to avoid punishment, she's still using subjectivism because avoiding trouble is still the most important outcome for her.

So, there you go. She can choose to keep the money or return it using the same ethical framework: *subjectivism*. Now, let me remind you again, hardly does anyone think about an ethical framework by name, before or after their choice. The decision is made, the action taken and we can examine those choices by unconsciously using these frameworks. We rarely use fancy, philosophical labels such as *subjectivism* to qualify our actions. Instead, we just feel right or struggle to feel less wrong about our choice, attempting to assuage our guilt by rationalizing. Our justifications will always fall into one or more of these five general Isms.

Here's another Ism using the same situation. Let's say after Grace discovers the extra $20, she decides to ask a friend if she should take the money back or keep it. In this case, for Grace, she will follow her friend's advice because she wants to please someone she considers important or close.

Grace doesn't have an answer on her own, so she's reaching out to her friend, part of her guild, (remember, a guild is an association of like-minded individuals). This ethical framework is called *Relativism*.

Grace's answer about whether to keep or return the money is not a universal yes or no, but rather it's relative to the standards of the group to which she belongs or wants to belong. If the advice from her friend is, "Take it back," she probably will. If the friend supports keeping the money, she will probably keep it or at least return it without telling her friend. Again, her ethics are relative to the standards of her friends. The problem with her relying on Relativism is that she can still come out with two opposite ethical decisions—both keeping the money or returning the money can each be ethical depending on the norms of her friends.

What if Grace doesn't take it back, but rather, gives it to a charity or to a homeless person on the street. She serves the greater good with her actions and isn't keeping the money for herself. This must be ethical, yes? *No!*

In giving the extra $20 to charity, she may be focused on the consequences of her actions, helping the needy, but this is still not taking an action based on universal principals. This is, by the way, the framework of *Consequentialism*—examining an ethical choice by focusing on its outcomes or consequences, rather than the action(s) being taken. In this case, Grace is focusing on the benefits to the needy rather than the fact she is utilizing the store's money without their permission or knowledge. Resources to the marginalized—ethical! Not keeping money that is not hers—ethical! Utilizing resources she does not own without permission from the actual owner who has the right to control their use—not ethical! If Grace focuses on the results and not her actions, she can feel ethical even when she is not. This is one form of *Consequentialism.*

Another form of *Consequentialism* has Grace returning the money for other reasons. She believes the money ensures that the company stays profitable and employees keep their jobs. Or the bumbling store clerk won't get fired and his family stays fed. These are consequentialist rationalizations. But as with subjectivism, and relativism, we have another ethics framework that argues two opposite actions can be ethical: keep the money or return it— whichever serves the greatest good.

## Intentions and the Isms

Participants at my talks often ask if we can understand someone's ethics by examining their intentions. Even in poor outcomes, if a person has the intention of an ethical result, weren't they in fact being ethical?

Discerning another person's honest intentions is near impossible. For instance, in the simple and ethical act of me giving a friend a birthday present, am I 100 percent certain of my own intentions? Do I give the gift for the joy of the recipient? Do I give it to demonstrate my love or connection with them (which may have more to do with me than them)? Do I give it because, having given them a gift last year, I need to fulfill their expectation about a gift this year? Do I give them a present because I expect a reciprocal birthday gift from them next year? Is it all of these intentions? Is it none of these intentions? How do I know? How would my friend know?

Even where the basis of law relies on discerning a defendant's intentions, we assign a judge and 12 jurors the task of listening to a litany of facts. While evidence helps determine guilt or innocence, it is still not providing us 100 percent certainty of someone's intentions.

No, intentionality may be the least effective perspective to use in understanding others and even our own ethics. Just remember the ancient proverb, "The road to hell is paved with good intentions." By the way, I say that with all good intention.

## Clearing the Air

No wonder people feel ethics are cloudy. A solid framework for decisions shouldn't allow all behaviors. Ethics are supposed to prohibit some actions and support others. Right and wrong are supposed to be black and white issues—and yet these frameworks keep us in the grey.

This realization led me to ask the question that precipitated my six years of dissertation research: why do good people make poor choices? Does knowledge about moral frameworks such as subjectivism, relativism, consequentialism and the others assist us in making ethical decisions? Or do they muddy the water? Do those who have formal ethics training grounded in these Isms make better choices? If our current conversations, education and training in ethics don't help us to make consistent "right" choices, what does? I pondered long and hard about how to scientifically discover the answers to these questions. I would never put someone into situations where good and bad choices had real consequences. That kind of research itself is unethical. Imagine getting volunteers to make harmful or unethical decisions where they believe the outcomes are real just to gain research data.

It's worth taking a moment to highlight this exact type of experiment and its consequences. In 1963, Psychologist Stanley Milgram at Yale University conducted research to measure levels of human obedience to authority. His test subjects believed they were administering electric shocks to anonymous recipients in the next room as punishment for giving wrong answers to verbal test questions. The shock recipient was playacting. Unaware of this, the participants dispensing the electricity were being guided by an actor in a doctor's white smock (the authority). The test subject was under real pressure to keep increasing the voltage with each wrong answer. They were, in fact, experiencing all of the actual emotions of a real situation in order to be accurately recorded for the research.

The researchers knew that authenticity was essential to discovering the impact of authority on our actions. This type of experimentation on humans is now illegal and was always unethical. Parenthetically, it is worth noting for this book that Milgrim's research methodology was justified as ethical, based on consequentialism. The researchers, ignoring the means—that is, placing subjects in predicaments with real emotional consequences—focused on the ends: obtaining authentic data measuring true obedience levels.

Research using live experiments with faux-ethical consequences wasn't even in my lexicon. I also knew I couldn't ensure truthful answers from face-to-face discussions about people's experiences. Our processes to make good and bad choices can be very personal. I could expect anyone I surveyed to overplay their good choices as a reflection on their character. Whatever research I did, there had to be anonymity so the responses would be honest.

My answer: I wound up surveying over 130 university students and corporate managers, some of whom had received formal training in the Isms and some of whom had not. After their training was completed, I had them fill out a personal ethics survey, *The Defining Issues Test* (DIT) published by The Center for the Study of Ethical Development at the University of Minnesota. This test has been used around the world with great statistical significance—a requirement for my dissertation.

The DIT poses ethical questions about five, short real-world scenarios, each with four responses that covertly reflect the Isms. Individuals choose what they see as the best response to each quandary. Their preferred moral frameworks are nestled inside their choices.

In examining the similarities and differences in their preferred answers, I separated participants who had been exposed to formal ethics education or training from those who had not. Before the survey was performed, I provided one third of the participants the standard Isms-based training, one-third of them an alternative training and one third of them no training.

To my shock, it turned out the group who had received the more common Ism-based training made lower level moral choices on the DIT test than the groups who had received no formal ethics training and those who received my proprietary training. Put simply, the results show that mainstream ethics training empowers less ethical choice-making. Imagine that! Most training and education on this vital subject is aiding us to make worse choices!

But why?

It turns out, the answer lies in the way we trainers train and educators educate—in essence, the conversation is the thing. As I had suspected but could not prove until I had this reliable data, we need a paradigm shift in the ways we examine and enable ourselves to make good choices. The old Ism-based conversations and teachings aren't doing this.

I'm not saying there are not other variables that impact our ethical decision-making. Other research shows situations, economic circumstances, religious traditions, family nurturing and much more affect what we believe to be right or wrong. What I am saying is that unless we take into account our capacities to morally advance and understand the potential limitations of the old philosophies and frameworks, we will retain our current state of ethical confusion. We must examine morality and ethics through new lenses.

The necessary shift to make better choices includes a clear understanding of our capacity to morally advance. Without that understanding, we hang on to the small t-truth that all ethics are grey.

The capital T-Truth is that moral standards are universal; that's what makes them moral and our actions are either ethical or unethical on that universal basis. Grey comes from the complexity of the circumstances and our perceptions around them. In three words: ethics are **black and white.** In fifteen more words, we have the capacity to morally progress past where we are now and do better.

• • • • • • • • • • • • • • • • • • • • • • • • • • • • • • • • • • •

## INSTANT REPLAY

**Guilds**: groups of like-minded individuals with similar interests or pursuits toward a common goal

**Subjectivism**: all ethical actions bring benefit to the choice-maker. An ethical choice provides gain or avoids punishment.

**Relativism**: all ethical actions can be judged on how closely they are aligned with group or guild agreements, norms of behavior, rules or laws. An ethical choice meets the expectations of those to whom the choice-maker is or wants to be connected.

**Consequentialism**: all ethical actions can be judged from the perspective of their moral outcomes. An ethical choice often maximizes the greatest good for the greatest number of stakeholders.

• • • • • • • • • • • • • • • • • • • • • • • • • • • • • • • • • • •

*Ethics Principle No. 12: The capital T-Truth is that moral standards are universal; that's what makes them moral, and our actions are either ethical or unethical on that universal basis.*

As we explore the Isms more deeply in the next chapters, we'll rely on one common scenario. You'll see in the grey box at the end of each section how the ethics of each perspective allow us to justify our choices. You can wait to read through the explanation of each framework first, or skip to the end of each section and view the different justifications.

Either way, I hope this next example helps personalize what can be a rather philosophical discussion.

On to what I have found to be a globally shared ethical quandary about earning grades at school.

## The Grade A Conundrum

Assume you are a student in one of my classes. You take the final exam and I have just returned it back to you graded. You earned 80 out of 100 total points, or an 80 percent, which is a B- or (2.7) grade. You had hoped for better, but at least you passed the course. Yay!

As you review the test, you notice something very peculiar. When I added up your final score, I made a math error. I shorted you 10 points because of a mistake in my addition, (a 2 + 2 = 3, sort of thing). If you add the 10 points back, you achieve that 90 percent and an A- (3.7) in the class. This is what you had hoped for! Double Yay! Immediately after class, you come running to my office, test paper in hand, so you can point out my math error. You want those 10 points! You've made an ethical choice and told me about the error. And to your relief, I also make an ethical decision, admit my error and re-record your correct score, giving you back your 10 well-earned points. The A- is yours. All is right with the universe. Problem solved, with a little help from the truth and an ethical ethics professor.

Now, let's change things up a bit. You get that same graded test back at the end of my class and it shows you passed with the 90 percent you had hoped for. (Triple Yay!) But as you go through and review your answers and my grading, you find I made a math error. But this error wound up giving you 10 more points than you actually earned, (a 2 + 2 = 5, sort of thing). Your true score is 80 percent, a B- for the class. *Now*, what do you do? I'm guessing, if you're like me, you are at least pondering about what not to do. Do you say nothing and keep the A- or do you identify the problem to me and get the B-?

Using truth when it benefits us and ignoring truth when it does not is the ultimate ethical gaff. The truth is the truth. The way we use it, if inconsistent, creates the ethical grey areas that muddy the rights and wrongs in our lives.

By the way, if you want to start an interesting discussion about ethics, pose this conundrum to your friends or colleagues and wander through the different ethical perspectives together. Our seeking the best grades in school is a universal experience.

Now, on to discover more about the Isms to see what they tell us about our ethical choices and this *Grade A Conundrum*.

# SUBJECTIVISM

*Me, Myself and I Decide What's Ethical*

*"I count him braver who overcomes his desires*
*than him who conquers his enemies;*
*for the hardest victory is over self."*
                                        *—Aristotle*

The Subjectivist approach to evaluating ethics maintains that individuals have the sole right to judge what is good or bad, right or wrong, for themselves. No one else can determine this as our independent judgments are based on both our rational thoughts *and* our personal feelings.

We can see a great example of this subjective, me-centered thinking in our individual choice of music—say, classical, pop, reggae, heavy metal, or opera. Musical taste isn't quantifiable by number of words, syncopation or note complexity. Rather, our preferences for songwriters, singers, bands and musical genre come from their very qualitative or emotional impacts on us. We love the music that moves us.

Subjectivists say the same thing about our ethical choices. Like our taste in music, we are moved to make our choices, ethical or not, based on the way they make us feel. A Subjectivist tries to maximize good feelings and minimize bad feelings.

Here's an example, courtesy of our friend Grace.

## Grace's Subjectivist Choices

**The moral**: Ethical choices sometimes require sacrifice. This may not always lead to positive feelings for the decision-maker, but it should always lead to positive feelings for those affected by the decision-maker.

 **The scenario**: Grace donates money to charity. Each time she does, she is careful to get a receipt for her tax deductions. The donation feels good and so do the tax savings. She also makes sure to let her friends know her immense pride in donating. That makes her feel good, too. Most of all, she likes helping people; that makes her feel the best. Subjectivism tells us that Grace's good feelings are the reason she does this ethical act. It doesn't take anything away from her altruism. Her feelings are driving her actions, just as her feelings drive her choices in music. Subjectivism defines that every ethical act is driven by the way we feel about it. Here's a slightly different example to provide some balance.

Grace sometimes parks her car in empty handicapped parking spaces when the lot is crowded and she's in a rush. This convenience allows her to maintain her busy schedule, shop easily and minimizes her exposure in bad weather.

Even though she is inconveniencing the handicapped and violating the parking laws, Grace feels good about these choices. If she didn't, she wouldn't make them. As a Subjectivist, she minimizes her guilt by feeling good about the other outcomes. When and if she has bad feelings, she'll change her behavior. Subjectivists say we cannot judge her good or bad feelings, only what her actions might do to others. Only she can judge her own feelings.

For instance, what happens to her feelings if she gets a parking ticket for this violation? Well, if there are enough good feelings despite the ticket, she'll keep parking illegally. It's like getting a speeding ticket. For most of us, speeding feels good enough to ignore the ethical considerations about violating the law. Even after getting a ticket, we may slow down for a time, but our speed creeps back up because that good feeling outweighs the risk of the bad feelings in another ticket. If we slow down permanently after the ticket, subjectivism says we are obeying the law, not for the law's sake, or even for others' safety, but because we feel better slowing down than we do risking another expensive ticket.

Simply put, even if it's illegal, we feel good speeding. And by the way, perhaps it's not the high speed itself we are choosing, but outcomes such as maximizing control over our own lives, maintaining our busy schedules, arriving at work or home predictably, ensuring we're not late, etc.

If Grace feels bad about the illegal parking after being ticketed, she'll hesitate to do it again. But if the good feelings from parking in the handicapped spaces are not overcome the bad ones, she'll be back in those spaces for her reasons in no time.

If she feels bad enough, say, for example, she is shamed by a person who could have legally parked in the space, perhaps she won't ever risk feeling *that* bad again and she will permanently change her illegal parking habit. Either way, she sees all of her choices as ethical because she feels good about their outcomes. That is subjectivism.

If you've ever had that moment in a full parking lot where the empty handicapped spaces were beckoning, then perhaps you have gone through this subjectivist thinking as well.

For illustrative purposes, let's assume Grace is an assistant at Worser and Worst Legal Advisors (WWLA). In the course of her work, she takes business trips, handing in monthly expense reports to get reimbursed for her costs. She is padding these reports with expenses she doesn't actually have so she can pocket the extra money. In other words, she gets just a little extra cash each month from adding a bit of fluff (that's a technical term) to her expense report.

Sometimes, she turns in a receipt for a big client dinner that shows a big tip when she actually didn't give one. She pockets that extra money. On other occasions, she buys gas for her family car and turns in a receipt to the firm showing the gas was part of a business trip in her company vehicle. She pockets, or rather tanks, the gas for herself.

She justifies these actions because she feels her salary at WWLA is too low and her work hours are too long. Whether she knows it or not, she is using subjectivism to justify financial fraud. She is taking care of herself because she feels these actions are the fairest way to adjust the wrongs of her hard work and low pay. Of course, there are ethical ways to make up for her low salary, such as talking to her boss and making the ask, or taking on some overtime, or a second job or even quitting and working elsewhere. But for her, the extra cash from this risk makes her feel better than the alternatives. Plus, she has probably minimized both the risks of getting caught and their consequences. If work policies change and the risk of getting caught increases, then her worry about being discovered may exceed her good feelings about extra cash and she'll change her actions to avoid the bad feelings.

Perhaps you're asking, "Why wouldn't Grace do more ethical things to feel better about her job?" While that's a great "Golden Rule" question, when individuals concentrate solely on themselves to weigh the ethical results of their choices, almost anything can be justified. Subjectivism can so easily go awry.

Let me provide a personal example. This is a true story.

## This is the Karma Bank, Right?

A few years ago, after doing some drive-through banking at my local Bank of WO, I noticed the teller had added an extra zero to my deposit. Instead of the actual $2,700 I had provided, the bank deposit receipt showed $27,000. Hmmm, a lucky break for me. How often does this happen?

Who wouldn't at least think of the possibilities? Why not proceed immediately to another branch of the same bank and withdraw that $27,000 recorded in my account. After all, this is obviously *karma*— what went around finally came around! The universe worked in my favor after so many years of seemingly being against me. Think of the wonderful things I could afford. Plus, I could feel good about using these 'extra' funds to take care of my family. I mean, this isn't intentional robbery . . . or is it?

What if they catch me as I'm withdrawing these misappropriated funds? Worse yet, what if they catch me after I've spent the money and they want it all back? What if taking money that's not mine is legally considered robbery? After all, I know the funds don't belong to me and I am acting like they do. All of this could get me in big trouble. Even if it isn't considered robbery, I am still withdrawing bank funds that belong to the bank.

Okay, how about I take the money, invest it in something short term while WO takes time to discover their error and trace it back to me. I'll reap the rewards of the investment interest and still have all of the funds to give back—short-term bonds anyone? This can't be robbery, can it?

All of these arguments and rationalizations streaming through my head for a few fiendish seconds are subjectivist arguments. My only thoughts about the ethics of taking this money are about the outcomes to me. That's subjectivism.

A far more ethical perspective goes beyond what happens to me and considers what happens to the actual owners of the money—the bank, its creditors and its depositors. None of my quick flashes of subjectivist justification consider them.

And what about the unfortunate teller? Surely, even if I could somehow rationalize that the bank can afford this 'minor' error, there is a good chance the teller will lose their job! I might even rationalize that keeping their money will teach the bank and this inept teller a lesson that will prevent this from ever happening again. The problem with this rationale is that I can accomplish the same thing without taking the money. All I have to do is step into the bank and show the manager the error.

Crime-fighter Chris to the ethical rescue!

Keeping this money can be rationalized as ethical as long as I ignore the outcome to others. And this is one of the great weaknesses of subjectivism. Unless I have some good or bad feeling myself about what happens to others, I don't take their results into account.

Just to finish this bizarre bank story: I didn't discover the teller error for three days. I innocently signed on to my account to pay a bill and discovered I had well over $27,000 in my account. I looked up my deposit receipts and sure enough, there was the teller's error. After a few seconds of subjectivist rationalizing and dreaming about the lifestyles of the rich and famous, I stepped up the moral ladder, called the bank branch and gave them the news. Now, the story really gets twisted.

Did you know you have to provide evidence to a bank that their record of any deposit is wrong? Their records show I deposited $27,000—I needed to *prove* to them I had not provided that amount. Think about that. How do you prove to a bank you did not give them money? Sure, they have the check somewhere in their archives, but they want immediate evidence from me. All I wanted was to be crystal clear I had nothing to do with this error. Talk about raising the ethical threshold on someone trying to do the right thing! It would have been less work for me to admit I was wrong. All I have to say is, "Oops, you're right. My mistake. How silly of me. I actually *did* give you $27,000. Sorry for the call. My bad—I must have fallen asleep in the car that day!"

The ending of this saga was that after two weeks and without any notice, my account was suddenly minus $24,300, (that's the $27,000 less my original $2,700 – at least they got that right). I had had over a two-week length of time to tumble around my subjectivist, self-serving and highly enriching options. Thank goodness subjectivism doesn't run in my family.

As you can see, being subjective in ethics can be very self-serving. But for Subjectivists, this is okay. In fact, they would argue all choices are made on the basis of personal gain. They believe that even the most charitable of behaviors originate from a self-serving motive.

Despite its self-serving nature, there is one component of ethical subjectivity worth carrying into a new understanding of ethics: **not all positive results can be measured tangibly**. Allowances must be made for weighing the emotional and spiritual gains and losses of our choices. Sometimes feeling good about our actions drives good ethical decisions. What does it matter that I want a tax write-off or recognition for making a hefty donation to my local charity? What does it matter if I follow the speed limit because I want to avoid a ticket? What does it matter if a person stops at a stop sign because he or she is fearful of an accident? The important and ethical thing is that they stopped.

What we discover with subjectivism is that a person using this framework does not *always* make the ethical choice. They make the choice that makes them feel good. There is a guarantee that ethics driven by self-satisfying behaviors will, at some point, break down and be used to make a wrong choice—the pull-me-up by pushing-you-down, kind of choice.

> *Ethical Principle No. 13: Allowances must be made as we weigh our ethical choices for our emotional and spiritual gains and losses.*

• • • • • • • • • • • • • • • • • • • • • • • • • • • • • • • • • • • •

## INSTANT REPLAY

**Subjectivism**: all ethical actions bring benefit to the choice-maker. An ethical choice provides gain or avoids punishment

**Rationalization**: attempting to explain or justify an action or an attitude through logical reasoning even when the behavior or attitude are emotionally based and negatively impactful to others

**Justification**: providing an explanation or excuse that an action or behavior is morally acceptable

• • • • • • • • • • • • • • • • • • • • • • • • • • • • • • • • • • • •


## The Flip Side of Me, Myself and I

There are some very dark ramifications to choosing ethics on the basis of personal feeling. As stated earlier, for better or worse, ethical subjectivity views emotional motivation as basic to all ethical choices. From this perspective, ethics boils down to an emotional quotient, rather than some level of rationality.

Because feeling outcomes are important in subjectivity, individuals with this mindset tend to utilize their own specific moral standards for their choices. This quite literally means that being ethically subjective allows anyone to qualify nearly any choice as ethical if it creates positive feelings in them. This perspective explains how Grace can justify padding her expenses. The behavior is wrong, even illegal, but the basis for justification is positively self-serving.

The subjective basis for ethical decisions can also be affected by an individual's circumstances at the time of the choice—their upbringing, personal economy, social class, levels of professional and personal discretion, faith perspectives, etc. A wide variety of influences makes ethical subjectivity far from universal in its application. Poor circumstances can be used to justify poor ethical choices. As we've noted, subjectivism suggests that what's right for one individual may not be right for another. In an ethical sense, my positive feelings about a choice are no better or worse than your positive feelings about a choice. This is a real problem if our choices lead to completely opposite actions.

For instance, if I'd kept that bank money, I could have justified it as ethical in a number of ways. Let's say you experience the same teller-error at your bank except you feel better about returning it, so you do. My action of keeping the money because it feels good and your action of returning the money because it feels good can't both be ethical. It is one or the other. Certainly, if we leave subjectivism behind and focus on the bank's feelings, it's the other. Giving the money back is the right thing to do, regardless of our feelings.

## Problems with Subjectivism

To be a bit academic for a moment, there are three very specific reasons that ethical subjectivism is a very limiting way to make ethical choices:

1. **There are unacceptable consequences to relying solely on subjectivism.** Under scrutiny, all behaviors become ethical if the principles chosen are logically arguable and the focus is on the feelings of the choice-maker.

    From individuals to organizations to entire nations, subjectivism allows for self-serving, even illegal decisions void of empathy and compassion. Cheating on taxes is an example. Government politics is full of the rationale that actions ensuring 'my' re-election are the ultimate best-practices for serving constituencies. Good feelings abound, but so do bad choices.

2. **This framework allows for arbitrary ethical choices that depend only upon the values of the person applying their own principles.** Since, as was stated earlier, humans have a

tendency toward self-centeredness, individuals often feel their own principles are good. I already reported that most people attending my seminars are there because they suspect the ethical motives of the folks around them and shy away from an examination of their own 'high' standards.

I have an anecdote about this. I noticed a substantial increase in my leadership consulting work after Congress passed the Sarbanes-Oxley Act in 2002. This legislation holds top executives accountable for the actions of their employees. It was passed in response to multiple CEOs, including those at ENRON, testifying before Congress that they had no awareness of what was happening in their companies because their subordinates never informed them. Sure, the CEOs had signed financial reports, but that didn't mean they had all of the reports explained to them. In essence, they claimed to be victims of their unethical subordinates. Sarbanes-Oxley changed the ability to avoid responsibility and ended that excuse.

My business boomed after this because executives, now facing possible imprisonment and personal fines for signing falsified reports, were requesting ethics training for their lower level managers so they could trust them. Bottom line, these executives figured they themselves were ethical; they just weren't sure about their employees. Now that's a very subjectivist perspective. Nice try, but the largest shadow is still cast from the top.

3. **Being ethically subjective, personal values and not public debate can justify almost any behavior**. As J. Desjardin, a noted ethicist states, "Ethical principles for good must be evaluated in a public process. Public standards must determine what is good or bad for that public." Subjectivity concentrates on personal circumstances and cares little for any public forum overseeing potential consequences. To quote the cartoon character, Popeye, "I's feels what I's feels."

I am guessing that those of you who went through the 2008 Great Recession may have been affected, perhaps greatly, by companies who proliferated a subjectivist business ethic. Here's one example: a number of the largest financial institutions in the US—the gems of Wall Street, Morgan Stanley, Bear Sterns, Goldman Sachs, Merrill Lynch, AIG, and others—wittingly ignored investors and mortgagees by extending historic amounts of credit to consumers who had poor debt histories. How did they justify and profit from this risk? They charged hidden, extensive and arbitrarily high upfront fees and interest rates to these risky debtors. With high fees, these finance companies would do just fine even as the over-extended homeowners defaulted and lost their homes. Some of these financial institutions were bailed out by the U.S. government, afraid the collapse of the big guys would be the collapse of the economy. This is where the phrase "too rich to fail" got its reprise. The 2015 film, *The Big Short,* provides a unique look at this collapse.

Somehow, we have to widen our net about how to make the best and most consistent ethical choices. We may have to set our personal feelings aside to find a universal truth that works the same way for all of us. With that in mind, let's press on to examine the other Isms that often get in the way of exercising that universal standard.

One last thing. As promised for each of the Isms, here is how a Subjectivist might justify his or her choices in the *Grade A Conundrum* from the last chapter. Do I keep the unearned grade points or give them back?

## Subjectivism and the Unearned Grade Points

As a **Subjectivist**, what do you do when you discover you received more points than you deserved because of the teacher's math error in scoring your exam? (The *Grade A Conundrum*, part 1)

- Do Nothing—nobody else including the teacher knows about this. So, you gain the good grade and there is little chance you'll get into trouble. You feel good about this.
- Do Nothing—what goes around finally has come around. Karma has finally worked in your favor. Keeping the unearned grade is the reward for a lot of worse luck in the past. You deserve this!
- Do Nothing—this is good for you and your academic career. A higher GPA might get you a scholarship or even a good recommendation for a great job.
- Do Nothing—who's this going to hurt? It's just a grade in one class and nobody will know, so you won't lose any friends which could make you feel bad.
- Inform the Teacher—he may know about this already and you could get in trouble.
- Inform the Teacher—these points don't belong to you. It's the honest thing to do and you feel better about honesty than you do about lying.
- Inform the Teacher—if you do the right thing, the teacher might let you keep the points. In that case, you've done the right thing *and* gained all the advantages doing nothing except the guilt. Wahoo!

The bottom line: when anyone can use the truth when it works in their favor but ignore the truth when it works against them, they are using subjectivism to justify the paradox. The major failing of the subjectivist perspective is that ethical right or wrong is entirely up to the individual based upon his or her own principles, diverse circumstances and feelings. Completely opposite choices can be ethically justified. This makes it too self-serving and limited for any universal ethical code.

# RELATIVISM

*Guilds and Allegiances Tell Us What's Ethical*

*"Associate yourself with people of good quality,*
*for it is better to be alone than in bad company."*
—*Booker T. Washington*

The single greatest problem with ethics today is the widely accepted and well-practiced principle that our ethics are relative to something other than a set of universal principles.

Relativism is the determination of what's ethical on the basis of its relative truth. Where a subjectivism relies on how individuals feel about an ethical choice, relativism concentrates our ethical decision-making around what is acceptable to those with whom we are affiliated. The "we" in this case can be informal group as small as two family members or friends or co-workers, or a group as large as an entire organization or community or nation. At any size, the guild is who we want to belong with.

## The Role of Guilds in Ethical Decision-Making

As I defined earlier, any group of like-minded individuals who in pursuit of common goals decides what behaviors are proper or improper, moral or immoral is a *guild*. A guild often qualifies its actions using an "us versus them" mentality. We are this guild, we do this. They are that guild, and they do that.

It is important we don't conclude guilds are made up only of the unethical. As a matter of fact, we give our allegiance to important guilds that provide sound ethical footings. We call them nations, regions, states, counties, cities and neighborhoods.

We operate in business guilds, sports guilds, church guilds, club guilds, school guilds, fraternity and sorority guilds and so many more. These are normal collectives of people who come together around agreements about who they are and what they can and cannot do when operating together. We often look at others' guilds with an exclusionary set of lenses. Dare I say, we can live with the "we versus them" mindset very easily when we are inside our own guild. A great example of this can be seen with sports-team fans. This is who we root for rain or shine. This is how we do the rooting. These are the teams we like and these are the teams we disdain.

It is natural, but often counter-productive, to maintain a guild mentality at all costs. Democrats and Republicans are a rich example of the behavior exclusive to one guild as it conflicts with another. And we see the result: the "us versus them" conflict takes on more meaning than the primary responsibility to govern for all of us.

We can see our own national guild mentality in reactions to events such as 9/11. Consider a well-known quote from that time justifying our response to this national tragedy: *"We have the duty as the freest nation on earth to take out these evil regimes."* I am not debating the right or wrong of those words, just highlighting their inclusiveness (who's in the guild) and their exclusiveness (who's out of this guild). So, a few guild questions, if I am allowed.

**Who assigned us this destructive duty?** Well, we did. We assigned ourselves this duty. It was not an active call from many outsiders. In fact, unlike the earlier 1990 Gulf War where our leadership role had been mandated by the United Nations and shared by many countries, we dove into the 2003 Iraq conflict against U.N. directives and accompanied by only four allies: the UK, Australia, Spain and Poland.

**Who qualifies us as the "freest nation on earth?"** Well, our guild does. I'm not sure *how* we qualify as "freest." I do know that there are many countries that have the same or even wider freedoms of democracy and open markets: Canada, Japan, Great Britain, Sweden and many others around the globe. I'm not sure how to measure the qualifier, "*freest* nation on Earth." I do suspect this is an empowering label meant to be publicized inside and outside the guild, especially as enemies are identified with labels such as fanatical tyrants who rob us of freedoms.

**Who qualified their guild as evil?** Well, our guild did. Perhaps there are a few others. I can say with certainty the "evil" guild does not label themselves that way. And from their actions before and after 9/11, we know some in that guild qualify *us* as evil.

When this "evil regime" label was used only days after 9/11, we had little understanding about the source or size of this terrorist conspiracy. If there is 'evil' in that guild, is it the entire population or just a few rotten eggs in their government and military?

Humans act most like an exclusive guild when they take unilateral actions against outsiders. Not to belabor this quote, let me switch it up a bit. Can you picture the 9/11 terrorists of the Iraqi guild justifying their actions in a mantra nearly the same as ours? The chant, "We have the duty as the most religious nation on earth to take out this evil regime," is eerily similar to the American version.

[If it is of interest, there is a dramatic speech by actor Jeff Daniels, portraying fictional anchorman Will McAvoy on *The Newsroom*, that speaks directly to the U.S. disabusing itself of certain guild mentalities. He's answering the question, "Why is America the greatest country in the world?" Some language may be offensive, but his answer, written by Aaron Sorkin, may surprise you. It is an interesting example of how a guild can create its own image and how maintaining that image shapes its relationship to the truth. Search *Will McAvoy America Best* on YouTube.]

## Positive Examples of Guilds

There are positive examples of guilds. I'll choose a guild to which almost half of all American adults have belonged: a jury.

Juries are tasked with finding the facts (knowledge) and then assigning guilt or innocence based on those facts (wisdom). While these are often very short-lived guilds, they are made up of individuals sharing a common purpose who are instructed to bring the aforementioned pillars of wisdom into their deliberations. According to *Advocates News*, a publication of this nation's leading jury and trial consulting firm, 44 percent of adult Americans have attended jury duty and 24 percent of us have actually been selected to sit on a jury. That's a hefty number of us exposed to the workings and morals of this particular guild.

How many just decisions come out of these guilds? Well, 53 percent of us say a jury is fair while only 26 percent of us feel a single judge is fairer. While I cannot argue that wisdom always prevails with juries, these statistics tell us we perceive that a guild made up of our peers following universal principles can be potent force for ethical choice-making.

## Guilds and Relativism

Relativism holds that there are no capital T-Truths, only small t-truths held by the guilds to which we belong. Where the group's ethics are not explicit, what you observe in the behaviors of those included and excluded from your group informs you about what is right and what is wrong. What those who practice relativity accept—wittingly or unwittingly—is that different moral standards can be practiced by different groups and still lead to ethical choices. But through this lens, anything is ethical if it is the norm of your guild.

Relativism is consensus-based ethics. Quite simply, this is the "When in Rome, do as the Romans do" approach to morality. Perhaps it's appropriate to illustrate relativism using our trusty friend, Grace and me.

## If the Shoe Fits

**The moral**: A sense of belonging is a powerful, ethical motivator. Group pressure and the desire to be included have great impacts on our morality that are difficult to perceive from inside the group. The group mentality and norms only further the feeling of a collective moral standard for even the worst ethical actions.

 **The scenario**: Grace is considering buying several pairs of inexpensive, faux-label shoes during her vacation to Asia. She can easily bring them back into the U.S. in her luggage. Who's going to know? The Asian country allows these faux-brand, high-end shoes and many other false products to be sold cheaply in their marketplaces. So, what's the harm? After all, she's following the rules in one country even if it violates the laws of her own country. Who is she to bring her own country's laws and moral codes to bear in another country—especially if this is how workers and shopkeepers in that country earn their living? Plus, she benefits fashion-wise in buying duplicates that no one can discern from the expensive originals. Everyone wins!

Not quite. In case it isn't already obvious, all of Grace's justifications fall under relativism.

Patent, copyright, trademark and registration laws around the world are meant to protect inventors and investors from copycats who profit from others' ideas and products. When cheaper copies flood the marketplace, original brands lose sales. This dynamic may never allow the original manufacturers to recoup their new product costs.

I wonder if Grace's choice for the faux shoes would be different if she had designed and marketed the originals herself? Or if her husband worked at a shoe factory being closed due to the growing sales of foreign, cheap copies? This would certainly answer her question about who gets harmed in these purchases.

I personally experienced this lesson when I was teaching and consulting in China over a five-year period starting in 2002. In my case it wasn't shoes—it was wrist watches. Watches can be far more expensive than shoes, so the temptation to save while boosting one's ego is even greater. After all, how could I ever afford or justify the $24,000 watches I was bringing home for just $29.99? And I must add . . . did they ever look good on my wrist.

My ethical error was brought home to me when I was sitting at a luncheon in Frankfurt, Germany, wearing one of my famous faux watches. The gentleman and his wife across the table from me noticed it right away.

"Oh, look honey," he observed, "Dr. Gilbert is wearing a beautiful Listmograph watch." (I made that name up.)

"Oh, yes," she answered. "I bought Jim his Listmograph for our 25th anniversary. I saved up for years! Isn't it fabulous—guaranteed to run forever and be only 1/1000th of a second off each century," she said to me.

"Why, yes," I sheepishly replied, as I remembered my faux had no guarantees and was already off by two minutes the first week I wore it. "Listmographs are great, aren't they? What a nice gift." I glanced at Jim's proudly extended arm.

"And see, Sweetie," Jim went on to point out, "Dr. Gilbert has the version with the titanium case and crystal-backed-pendulum-winder that we couldn't afford. That's just top notch!"

Ouch.

The real watch he wore was in the $16,000 range. I gulp now as I say it. The original version of the Listmograph he thought I had on was in the $18,000 range. The copy I was so effectively and affectively wearing, the upscale model they couldn't afford, had cost me a grand total of $41.99 plus no tax in China.

But wait, if you think I've shrunk in my seat as far as I can, here comes the *coup-de-gras*.

Jim asked, "Can I put your titanium Listmograph on for just a moment to see how light it is compared to mine? We figured the difference in weight just wasn't enough to make up for that price." He winked at me and quietly whispered, "It's how I justified keeping the less expensive version she bought me."

YOW! Need I go further?

All right, one more step. Here's the icing atop the coup-de-gras cake. Once Jim slipped my fake watch onto his wrist, he commented, "Wow, this is really light!"

Never mind it's lighter, not because of its titanium case, but because my faux has plastic parts and is made of cheap, thinner metal. What could I say to these dear people? I lost all faux-pride in wearing this copy. I felt like an _ss! This incident also caused me to think about the information I was hiding, the money I was "robbing" from the original watch manufacturers (a felony if I had actually stolen this amount in cash from them) and the pride I was faking in front of others who'd really budgeted and sacrificed to purchase such an expensive gift.

The relativism that justified the great bargain for Dr. Gilbert was based upon ignorance of justice and a violation of trademark and patent rights. I was fine following the ethic of the country that was ignoring the law. I was also fine with the ethic needed to fit in with the rich-watch set. Those moral standards of one guild shriveled at the point when another group I wanted to associate with prioritized honesty, the profits of a free market and the idea of sacrifice and gifting.

I still have that watch—I just don't wear it anymore. By the way, it quit working after three years. Serves me right.

There is one more interesting fact about the faux watch sales in China which may or may not extend to other faux goods. It turns out there were three levels of quality faux watches. The cheapest were the ones manufactured in China. These didn't resemble the originals very well, were often made of cheap metal that turned your wrist green over time and were priced at about $10. Then, there were the Japanese-made faux watches—better quality, better finish, and slightly more reliable inner workings. These might last a few years and cost around $25. Finally, there were the Swiss faux watches. These included copies of hundreds of exquisite Swiss designs. These highest quality fauxs were the most expensive— in the range of $30 to $90 for near-perfect, Swiss-made copies of $20,000 to $100,000 originals. My Listmograph was a Swiss copy faux. Why would Swiss companies make fake versions of their own manufacturer's watches? Because there is a huge international market of buyers who could never afford the originals but buy the faux watches in great volume. It's all about profit . . . only it's not!

## Bribery and Other Relativist Norms

There are leagues of ethical relativism issues that occur in international business dealings. Questions on bribery and buy-ins for marketplace access come up regularly in my corporate seminars. These usually center on the ethics of conducting business in the way other countries find acceptable or whether U.S. companies should bring the laws and morals of our own country into these business deals. The main question is often, "Don't the common practices of the country you're working with take priority if you want to join them in a full business relationship?" This is a perfectly relativist question, the answer to which is, "No!"

In this same conversation, I often inquire if there is a line these folks would draw if the host country was practicing an extremely wanton or illegal activity. Most often the answer is, 'Yes, they would draw a line.' I point out that, just like we can't be "sort of" ethical, one cannot be 'sort of' relativist. To practice relativism well is to accept all of the ethical choices of another group without judgment. Now that's fraught with peril, isn't it? At least this conversation gets people to think about the relativity of their relativism, and to examine at what point their own moral line stops them from accepting all behaviors.

In an older tale of international relativism, the once vast commercial aircraft division of Lockheed-Martin fell into the relativity trap decades ago. Faced with the choice of losing a multi-billion-dollar Japan Airlines contract for their wide body, L-1011 jets in the late 1980s or making a $44 million-dollar "good faith" payment to Japanese legislators controlling the deal, Lockheed paid the bribe. At that time, this was the way business was done in Japan. Once this action was uncovered however, the U.S. government levied fines and tripled the monetary damages on Lockheed, forcing the eventual closure of their entire commercial aircraft division. It's one of the reasons the only commercial aircraft manufacturer in the U.S. now is Boeing.

I highlight this incident because it gave teeth to the *U.S. Foreign Corrupt Practices Act*. This law stands completely opposed to the idea that ethics are relative to the country or culture in which you're doing business. It is the beginning of multiple rules recognizing universal standards inside a free-market system that ensure fairness to everyone. A system legitimizing bribery eventually cuts smaller businesses out of the marketplaces who, unlike richer firms can't afford to play the payoff game. Over time, capitalism itself crumbles in the face of a system that only rewards the biggest players.

Consider how unjust and inequitable a system of bribery is. Firstly, only those who can afford to bribe can play the game. Secondly, there are only two ways a company can raise money to pay the bribe. Either they must over-inflate the price of the item or they must cut back on the costs of manufacturing so that the final price covers the additional bribe money. Either way, customers are not getting what they were promised. They don't wind up paying a fair price for a quality good. Instead, they wind up paying the extra amount necessary for the bribes. In a bribery-ruled world, customers are overpaying for inferior quality.

Another personal (true) story may be useful here.

One of my college students with significant financial challenges visited my office one afternoon. He was taking my business ethics course and we were far enough into the quarter that we had already covered the Isms. He was asking me whether, in the service of his education, he should consider joining a gang that promised to provide money in exchange for their "jobs" in his neighborhood. I was surprised by the question; I had never considered the income from gang activities, legal or otherwise, would be used for positive ends such as education. That was a good lesson for me. I also understood that, at its heart, this was his struggle with the trade-offs between dropping out of college or putting in with a group following highly questionable ethics. I didn't ask him for the particulars. Instead, I concentrated on the gang's values and virtues compared to those of his family and college friends. I wanted to explore with him how well he could live into the extreme differences of these disparate guilds' opposing ethical standards.

Underneath, this was a conversation about relativism and its effect on the moral quality of his life. I asked him if he wanted his two younger brothers to join this gang. His answer was an emphatic, "No!" We spent several hours exploring the options. I felt my job wasn't to judge, but to accompany him through the tangle of relativist thoughts.

He had good questions. Weren't a few years of bad choices worth a lifetime of good ones? Couldn't he actually help the gang out of its ethical rut if he got involved? What if he kept a low profile and just completed the tasks that weren't that unethical or illegal? Wasn't the system that perpetuated the financial disparities between his neighborhood and the affluent ones really to blame for the gang's unethical behaviors? In other words, does this or any gang really have a choice in such a biased, social-class system?

While relevant, these questions cloud over the most important one. I focused him on this question: Is it ethical for any guild to decide for any reason to negatively impact the quality of others' lives for the guild's benefit?

To answer this question, I concentrated on the gang initiation rite he revealed he'd need to fulfill before he was accepted. Each prospective candidate had to steal something of value from a rival gang to prove his worth. My student was greatly concerned about the short and long-term outcomes of this task. On the basis that personalizing an ethical dilemma makes it easier to discern, I asked him what he'd do if the initiation right meant stealing from friends, or family members or his professor? I think that pushed him over the edge. He began to view the gang's ethic in light of the stakeholders affected by their actions. This is climbing a ladder out of the morass of relativist thinking toward moral high ground.

The gang didn't see itself as unethical. That may be hard to understand, especially as this type of guild breaks laws and worse. But as I stated before, no person or group sets out each day saying, "Let's be unethical." They find all the reasons that justify their ethic. And the group mentality and norms only further the feeling of a collective moral standard for even the worst ethical actions.

Group norms can be powerful to our higher nature and to our lower nature. Gangs and other groups practice their own ethics to provide protection, belonging, economic stability, substitute parental connections and so on. But if you believe in the mantra that "there's no right way to do the wrong thing," a gang's relativist ethic doesn't actually provide for the long-term needs of the members. Nor does it change the system that created it. Bad actions might lead to short term gains, but they always fail in the end.

My student eventually discovered this in his deliberations. He decided to join *our* gang, the gang of college educators and students, preferring to take lesser paying teaching assistant and internship positions and extending his course work an extra two quarters. Once he graduated, I'd like to believe that this and other experiences were what led him to join a gang intervention organization similar to Denver's Gang Rescue and Support Project (GRASP). They offer one-on-one mentoring, school presentations, the Unity Mural Project, gang tattoo removal, and other at-risk supports. This was a great outcome for my student and the lives of all he touched. And it came from the challenge of discerning right and wrong.

Group relativism is perpetuated by group norms—expected ways we behave. When faced with the threat of being an outcast or worse, we may alter our own ethic to conform to the group, even at the risk of participating in clearly illegal actions. Group pressure is a powerful ethics motivator and de-motivator.

I had another student who reported that her employer, a drug manufacturing company, was wrongly labeling its over-the-counter drug so it would be seen as less dangerous by consumers. There was intense pressure by her co-workers to let it go. As a single mother, to lose her job seemed even more dangerous, and yet, here she was reporting her struggle with this ethical conundrum to the entire class. After some very intense, private conversations with her, she came to the conclusion that the truth she knew was more important than the salary she received. She made the choice to quit and to report the company's activity. It was hard at first, but in the end, she left an immoral situation for much more ethical and lucrative work at a higher salary with a competitor. The defrauding company was eventually caught, closed and the complicit workers fired a year later. Her ethical stance based on the universal principles of trust and trustworthiness was richly rewarded.

While these happy endings may not appear instantly when everyone chooses right over wrong or goes against the grain of the group belief, there is a valuable lesson here. **You are the only person who has to look at yourself in the mirror every morning. Whom do you want to see there?** Sometimes the complexity of a tough ethical choice comes down to moral courage. And courage is not the absence of fear. Courage is taking an action despite the fear.

Relativism can be so insidious; it is worth spending a few more pages on it before we apply this ethical framework to our choices in the *Grade A Conundrum.*

# RELATIVISM, PART 2

## *The Pressures of Relativity*

*"We should challenge the relativism that tells us there is no right or wrong, when every instinct of our mind knows it is not so, and is a mere excuse to allow us to indulge in what we believe we can get away with. A world without values quickly becomes a world without value."*

—*Jonathan Sacks*

Ethical Relativists argue that all ethical choices are a product of our backgrounds, upbringing, education and our guilds. This means moral limitations on our behaviors are created and enforced by the groups that created them. And if you switch from one group to the next, you may have to accept different moral standards—sometimes exactly the opposite of your previous group's.

To raise ethical relativity to a societal level, certain countries still prohibit women's access to higher education on the basis of exclusive religious interpretations, societal norms and control of one gender over another. The nations that enjoy greater freedoms and recognize the equality of men and women but still continue economic relationships with these less equitable nations demonstrate relativism. As I have stated, if ethics are meant to tell us right from wrong while upholding universal standards, then relativism is a grave error in moral judgment.

There are growing trade policies and economic partnerships between nations that include incentives and disincentives targeted at minimizing injustices and inequities. Even with these, there is still some level of ethical relativism in trading with these partners, but at least they are forced to examine and even sometimes change their immoral standards and ineffective laws.

Although there are economic sanctions exercised around the world, this concept of fair-trade based on universal ethics may be a sore point for some. You may ask, "Who are we to impose our standards on someone else? Who gave us that heady responsibility?" My answer is this: if we boiled this international stuff down to something more personal, perhaps it crosses the ethical threshold and seems more accessible.

As an example, let us assume you regularly rented your car to your neighbor in exchange for cash. He uses your car with care, and even forces his young daughters to wash and wax it each time he drives. In fact, he keeps his girls out of school if necessary, in order to give you back a clean car. His boys are not responsible for the car and go to school every day.

Does he have a right to do this? Not by law; it's illegal to keep any of his children out of school in our gender-neutral system of compulsory education laws.

Do you have a duty to do something about this? According to the law, you should report it or you are complicit in the illegal behavior.

Forget the law for a moment. What about the ethics in this situation? What if the father prioritizes male over female education because of religious beliefs? If we apply universal principles that allow everyone to achieve their greatest capacity regardless of gender, this small t-based gender bias is unethical.

Does it matter how strongly the father believes in this prejudiced paradigm? No. Strength of belief does not define capital T-Truth. How could you, the car owner, make a difference? Without interfering in child rearing, family or religious values, you can create and enforce a set of rules that accompany the rental of your car—rules devised to support his children's right to education while still maintaining your valuable trade. Might you lose the transactions if he decides the rules are too restrictive? Yes, but in the long term, the higher moral value here is enforcing the ethics that provide equal access to the education mandated by law.

We can extend this simple example to the international exchanges that occur between trading partners. This is not always an easy task. In fact, I once had a boisterous discussion with several female students in my graduate ethics course about women's rights around the world. To my shock and horror, these mid-level, female executives working white collar jobs in the United States argued that if other countries believed women should not have equal access to education, jobs and other rights, who were we to impose our system on them? I pointed out that we weren't imposing our own relativist ethic on another country. We were enforcing universal rights due everyone. After all, who has the right to decide who can and cannot achieve their greatest capacities?

I am not sure this conversation led to a change in their perspectives as Relativist fundamentalists, but it sure opened my eyes to how relativist thinking can cloud the view of those whom I'd assumed, through their experience, education, position and *gender*, would have great affinity, compassion and empathy for these girls denied an equal education. In my faith, gender equality is looked at as two wings of the bird. The left and right wings are not the same, but unless both are unencumbered and pull equally, the bird never takes flight.

Another example of relativism in the trading partner world was Nike's outsourcing of shoe production in the mid-'90s to Asian Pacific countries practicing child labor. Nike executives made this short-lived decision under the mistaken belief it was a fair competitive practice. Since this form of injustice was acceptable in the factory host countries, Nike believed it ethically correct to ignore these conditions. Nike even rationalized its decision as contributing positively to the host countries' developing economies. Imagine what the answer would be if you requested those same Nike executives to send their own children over for factory work to help the country's underdeveloped economy. "Heck no!" would be an example of a mild response.

If what works over there won't work over here, but your actions ignore the difference, that is ethical relativism.

The current rise in sexual harassment accusations sweeping this country and other parts of the world is a hopeful example of the death of a relativist ethic. In the "old" days, abusive behavior was accepted in the entertainment industry. It was the cost of joining that guild and remaining in it. The cost of that immorality finally exceeded its benefits. The correct, capital T-Truth, that all of us deserve an equal chance based on our talents and capacities, and that no one is famous or influential enough to be excused from unethical and illegal behaviors, now vigorously displaces those individuals who practiced the old immorality.

> *Ethical Principle No. 14: If what is ethical for one group is not ethical for another, but interactions between the two ignore the difference, then ethical relativism deeply shades any hope of universal rights in both groups.*

Here's one final example of the downfalls of relativism that is still active in our own country today.

In the business world, gift-giving is still a normal process for developing professional relationships. The awarding of a big contract can be ensured beforehand through gifts and incentives to the contract's decision-makers. This has been seen as fair practice in the business world since organized business began. There are now gifting limits in some sectors, such as government, but gifting is not seen as creating inequity—it is seen as kindness, relationship-building and standard operating procedure.

Let us move this type of gifting into the academic world—the education guild. Why are gifts between students and their professors not standard practice in education? (I could afford that genuine, Listmograph if it was!) Somehow, in academia, it is easier for all to see the undue influence a student's gifts might have on the professor's grading practices. And even if there were no actual influence in a gift, how could the professor or student ever prove to anyone it had not impacted grading?

Perhaps, in the world of education, it's easier to see the great imbalance between the students who can afford to give professors gifts and those who cannot. Should rich students have a better chance at a higher grade than financially challenged students? I am assuming you're saying no to all of the above because you recognize the inequity and injustice in an educational system that prioritizes rewards for the professor's favors over a truthful evaluation of the student's mastery of information. Suffice it to say, gifting by students to their teachers is a norm in some countries.

Aren't all of the questions about the fairness of student gifting relevant to the issues of business gifting? Yes. Should a contract be granted to a supplier on the basis of gifts and favors, or on the basis of the best quality for the best price and service? Should businesses rich enough to provide gifts to clients or potential clients have better access to contracts than smaller 'Mom-and-Pop' operations? In an ethical world, shouldn't all gifts be turned down by recipient organizations to avoid undue influence or the appearance of undue influence?

I worked with a large timber and paper producer in the Northwest that was wrestling with these questions in the '90s. It did a lot of international business and traveling salespeople received many gifts—some very expensive, such as antique Asian suits of armor and thousand-dollar bottles of wine. The company was looking for a policy that allowed them to accept the gifts without any *individuals* benefitting from them. They wanted to accept in some way because there are business cultures that mandate such exchanges in relationship building. Our solution: allow the gift to be given anonymously. Store the gifts and hold an annual auction during the holidays where employees bid on these gifts and the proceeds of the auction go to the charities of their choice. This minimized the undue influence and provided a great venue for charitable donations. Employees also felt good about the deals they got at an auction benefiting good causes.

By the way, back in the world of academia, I tell my students if they feel compelled to give me a gift, they can give me anything they want as long as it is given to me anonymously. For some reason, I don't get many gifts. Why, you ask? Because despite someone's best intentions and their promise that they are not expecting anything in return, we all have expectations about the recognition of a thank you.

I should probably clarify that I am not in any way implying gift-giving between family and friends is unethical. This is a kindness and often expected. I *am* saying that gifts between those who have superior-subordinate relationships, such as vendors and suppliers, contractors and contractees, teachers and students, can never be truly free of undue influence and reciprocal expectations. Gifting in these cases should be assiduously avoided.

While gifting in government agencies, non-profits and many private sector organizations has slowly begun to fade, it does still occur and it is still widely accepted. Whether it's an expensive pen, a trip to the tropics, seats at a sporting event, new golf clubs, fine dining, etc., behavior in business seems to have a different moral standard than behavior in education and other arenas. Where we look at gifting in the business world and give the thumbs-up, and then glance at this habit in the academic world and flip a thumbs-down, that is relativism at its finest.

As I stated in the beginning, from my perspective, the greatest single problem in the practice of ethics today is the widespread acceptance of relativism as a legitimate framework for ethical decision-making. No other framework is as pervasive or as erosive of a sense of universal ethical principles or moral rights. This framework has the capacity for group justification of behaviors mutually exclusive to our basic responsibilities as humans to recognize our impacts on one another. Someone utilizing ethical relativity can argue that values such as equality, fairness, integrity, self-respect and freedom are themselves a matter of personal, group, organizational or national culture. In fact, J. Desjardins points out, "Relativism represents a serious challenge to ethics . . . because if it is correct, there is no reason to continue (the) study of ethics. If all opinions are equally valid, then it makes little sense for us to attempt to evaluate ethical judgments."

> ### *Ethics Principle No. 15: Trustworthiness leaves little room for relativism.*

## What if My Guild Is Wrong?

Among the host of ideas already discussed, there are three specific reasons that ethical relativism is both limiting and antithetical to universal moral standards:

1.  **Relative choices are not permanent.** They change over time, with cultures, changes in guild leadership and membership, current events and so on. This would support the erroneous assumption that ethics do not protect universal rights; they can change from place to place or time to time. If you consider such practices as child labor, theft, bribery, sexual harassment,

prejudice, etc., aren't these all equally unethical in Africa, Central America, Europe, the U.S. or any other nation on the planet? Ethics everywhere, while reflective of the current, moral development of any particular guild, are nonetheless supposed to be a consistent guide to a moral world. They protect the universal rights of every human being. The ultimate ethical question is not, have we protected or advanced our guild, but is this the right choice for everyone affected?

We see echoes of the answer to this question in the passage of the U.S. Civil Rights Act of 1964. This law prohibited previously widespread cultural norms legitimizing prejudice and segregation. The unequal treatment of African Americans and other minorities justified for centuries in this country has, over time, been reset towards more ethical behaviors. We have a ways to go, but universal causes of equity and justice triumph over those established for self-serving, exclusive guilds every time.

2. **Under relativism, all opinions are valid.** While ethical relativism acknowledges that any society is composed of groups and individuals with diverse views, differing opinions and opposing norms, the validity of all opinions does not work to create a universal set of ethical norms.

3. **If conditions of right or wrong change from time to time and group to group, then under relativism, *no* specific behavior can ever be judged as unethical.** The old saying, "When in Rome…", leads to an assumption that any action within a relativist consensus or norm can be ethical in the right place and under the right circumstance with the right group. To do as the Romans did would allow quite ethically compromising behaviors.

• • • • • • • • • • • • • • • • • • • • • • • • • • • • • • • • •

## INSTANT REPLAY

**Relativism**: all ethical actions can be judged on how closely they align with group agreements, norms of behavior, rules, or laws. An ethical choice meets the expectations of the others to whom the choice-maker is or wants to be connected

**Bribery**: giving something of value in exchange for an alteration of behaviors or outcomes

**Gifting**: the act of giving or bestowing something to a recipient often with expectations about reciprocal actions or recognition

**Universal Rights** (as informed by the UN Declaration of Human Rights): recognition of the inherent dignity and of the equal and inalienable rights of all members of the human family as the foundation of freedom, justice and peace in the world

• • • • • • • • • • • • • • • • • • • • • • • • • • • • • • • • •

Finally, below, you will find examples of how a Relativist might justify his or her choices about keeping or giving back those extra grade points.

### Relativism and the Unearned Grade Points

As a Relativist, what do you do when you discover you received more points than you deserved because of the teacher's math error scoring the exam? (The *Grade A Conundrum*, part 2).

- Do Nothing—all of my friends would agree it's crazy to give back these points.
- Do Nothing—I'm positive any other student who got such a 'blessing' would accept it quietly and move on with the better grade.
- Do Nothing—a good grade will allow me to get that scholarship and a better job so I can take better care of my family. I know they would agree!
- Do Nothing—my group loves a great, "fool the professor" story, this will earn me some points with my peers. Once I let my friends know about this, then I'll get some real respect.
- Do Nothing—the course syllabus says nothing about giving points back, so I'm not legally obligated to do it. We all agreed with the teacher at the beginning of the course to follow the syllabus.
- Inform the teacher—the guidelines of the school say you can't cheat and this is cheating.
- Inform the teacher—if my friends find out about this lie, they'll never speak to me again, I'm out of the study group, and no one will pick me as a team member in future classes.
- Inform the teacher—some of my friends are trying to get that scholarship and it's not fair to them that I get it with a false grade. I owe it to my buddies.
- Inform the teacher—the course syllabus clearly says to bring grading errors of any kind to the teacher's attention. I must follow the rules.

In the end, relativism's reliance on consensual opinion is fraught with peril since not all perspectives provide equal access to the capital T-Truth. Relativist ethics are poorly supported by small t-truths. In fact, if you think about it, the idea of relative truth is an oxymoron since small t-truth shared by members of the guild—be they friends, family, community, public or private sector organizations or an entire nation—can hide the benefits of the larger, universal truths equitable to all.

# CONSEQUENTIALISM, VIRTUISM, AND UNIVERSALISM

*Tell Us What Happened, It May Be Ethical!*

*"You are free to make your choices,*
*but you are not free to choose the consequences."*
—*Anonymous*

I was living in Russia in 1994, just after the Berlin Wall fell, working as the project director of a two hundred thousand-dollar United States Information Agency (USIA) grant in support of partnerships between colleges. My school was partnering with one of the first private colleges in the new Russia, Pskov Volny University. A significant portion of the grant money was dedicated to providing Volny educational resources, including textbooks, computers, a copy machine and other supports.

*Pskov Kreml, Pskov, Russia, 1994*

The ultimate objective was the planning and outfitting of an income generating, computerized business support and training center at the university. In fact, we had to get the U.S. government's permission to export one of the first Pentium computers into Russia. The Pentium used the first computer micro-chip sophisticated enough for pinpoint guidance systems in nuclear missiles. Since their purpose in our grant was far less nefarious, USIA signed off with the caveat we hire a military escort to safely transport these computers from the St. Petersburg airport to the college five hours away.

My overall experience on this project was wonderful and richly rewarding. I've already mentioned my friendships in a culture rich in connections and generosities. However, within weeks of beginning the work there, I ran into a big wall that would affect my professional experience and personally define for me our next Ism—*Consequentialism*.

The Volny perspective on the grant funds was that some money should be earmarked for the college's operating expenses. Books, computers and business centers were fine, but for them this was better chance at surviving a climate biased toward supporting the old Soviet State schools. Volny was perpetually starved for financial resources. Nearly every business in the city of Pskov, where I resided, seemed to be closed or closing. Empty apartments, abandoned buildings, half-completed restaurants and hotels, an aging infrastructure stressed to meet growing needs—the entire country seemed challenged by limited resources. As inflation was exploding and student funding for Volny was shrinking, all schools were among the worst victim of the shortfalls.

To provide some perspective on these dire economic straits, when I arrived in Pskov in 1994, the exchange rate was R2500 (rubles) to one U.S. dollar. By the time I left Russia a year later, inflation had doubled that original exchange rate to over R5000 to one U.S. dollar. Just two years after we were there, the exchange rate was over R25,000 rubles to one U.S. the dollar.

In such an imploding economic environment, it was easy to understand the pressures Volny administrators placed on me to covertly re-categorize grant expenditures and break USIA rules to get them cash. (This is a bit like Grace's padded expense report back when we were examining Subjectivism.)

Stymied, my Russian colleagues took verbal pressure a step further. Stonewalled by my stalwart belief in the grant's directives prohibiting cash donations to the college, Volny senior administrators hatched a clever way to get their money. Their methods meant chewing me up personally and professionally and the outcome would get them their funds. As we will soon see, people in survival mode can become very consequentialist-driven.

## The End Justifies the Means

This third traditional ethical framework, Consequentialism, concentrates on the end results of our choices to determine the ethics of our actions. In this view, right and wrong are judged by outcomes and not the means that are used to achieve them. Keep this in mind as I continue my tale of Russian unraveling.

An American translator hired for our grant project was not completing his work. His talents were vital to our interviews with Pskov businesspeople. After weeks of his inconsistent attendance and multiple conversations with me, I finally had to take him off the project and send him home. I hired a local Volny faculty member to finish his translation work. As it turned out, that change planted a seed in the Volny administration's mind about how they could get cash from the grant. My newly hired faculty translator was instructed by Volny to turn his compensation for grant work directly over to the college. He would get a small percentage of the total. With his teaching position at stake, he hesitatingly complied without telling me.

Meanwhile, the American translator, angry over his early departure, promised he would sue my school for breach of contract. Since I had already instructed my U.S. college to complete his payout, I was not too concerned. It turns out his plan was to leave that last paycheck uncashed and use this as the evidence we had stiffed him. This may seem crazy, but it's probably not an original idea. I tried to explain how our already recorded check would demonstrate we had fulfilled our side of the bargain. Still, he refused to accept this and it was at this point in our conversation I unwittingly planted the seeds of my professional demise.

An uncollected check was a waste of grant money, so I suggested to him that if he didn't want the money, he could donate it to Volny. He smiled and headed off to the airport.

Great idea, Dr. Gilbert! I was so proud. Small problem solved. Much bigger problem yet to come. Not only did he cash the final paycheck check and gift the money to Volny, he and the senior Volny administrator had discovered a sure-fire method for getting more cash indirectly from the Grant. Volny began pressuring me for more translation work. Since outreach to Russian businesspersons was complete, I did not understand their request. I had still not connected the dots.

This is where consequentialist thinking by my Russian and American comrades kicked in. As the Volny president visited my U.S. college on exchange, he and the fired translator, now home, raised questions at my school about grant mismanagement. They even hinted about financial fraud. Faced with an information vacuum while I worked remotely in Russia and with no reason to suspect ulterior Russian motives, my Grant Committee approved additional translator work. They also unceremoniously took away my project management responsibilities and ordered an immediate audit of all grant expenditures. When I got word of this by international fax, I was flabbergasted. This electronic communiqué was closely followed by a long telephone call from my Dean. My responses and explanations fell on deaf ears. I was instructed to finish my stay and organize a report about grant payments that accounted for every spent Ruble! I was beaten, but not defeated.

In the end, as I knew they would, the grant committee found nothing out of place. My expense reports and expenditures were squeaky clean.

By the time I returned to the U.S. in early July with my colleagues on summer break, the deed was done and the Volny president and translator were back in Russia with the extra money.

How did Volny get the cash? It's the last chapter of this near-spy story. The smokescreen of their false accusations about me diverted the grant committee's attention away from project work and toward "firefighting." With significant questions about my judgment hanging in the air and worried the program was somehow de-railing, they modified grant expenditures, restricted my access to the funds, and added an additional $15,000 dollars for continued (and unnecessary) translation work. With me living 10,000 miles away. Volny got their cash, I was sidelined and the grant project was completed a year later. Ends accomplished and the greater good was served.

Meanwhile, I, the heap on the ground, had the job of clearing my name while the perpetrators were now 10,000 miles away. My career and reputation were of little consequence to Volny. They got what they needed through their consequentialist ethic—the ends justifies the means! One person's besmirchment was irrelevant to the greater good of keeping 250+ students and faculty at an operating university.

This was one of the toughest ethics lessons I have ever faced professionally, and like *Cravings*, I am thankful. It added the necessary fuel to my devotion to understand better ethical choice-making.

## The Cost of Our Profits

There are myriad examples of various forms of Consequentialism in politics, education, sports, entertainment, religion, family relations and on and on.

A classic case of raw consequentialism was utilized by the Ford Motor Company in the early 70's with their decisions about Pinto automobiles. After a series of rear end collisions, explosions and fatalities, Ford choose not to replace an inexpensive fuel tank part in their Pintos. They conducted a cost-benefit analysis comparing the costs of replacing a twenty-dollar part in tens of thousands of cars to the cost of carrying insurance against wrongful death lawsuits from Pinto victims. The cost of carrying insurance insuring was cheaper. So, Ford left the fuel tanks unchanged.

In an economic equation, they justified the outcome of serving the greater good through cheaper cars, few inconvenient recalls and a profitable Ford. They demonstrated complete disregard for the potential victims of these preventable, fatal accidents. One hundred and seventy-seven fatalities later, Ford changed its policy and accepted the higher costs of Pinto gas tank repair and redesign. In the end, these accidents and the subsequent lawsuits based on Ford's faulty utilitarian thinking (that's a form of consequentialism based on cost-benefit analysis) cost them millions of dollars and caused the demise of the Pinto car line.

We repeatedly witness this type of faulty mindset. Pollution-control tampering conducted by Volkswagen Corporation to sell more diesel automobiles in the United States; short cuts on the Boeing 737 Max that cost hundreds of lives; Purdue Pharma and allegations of profiteering on the backs of the Opioid addicted, these are all examples of the same consequentialist ethic. Only now, the current cost of such unethical behaviors has climbed into the billions of dollars. Some say these companies may never fully recover. If only the Utilitarians in all these situations had added the costs of getting caught and prosecuted to the final outcomes. Perhaps then, the means would not justify the ends.

Quantitatively or qualitatively, if the result of a decision creates widespread, positive gains for the majority, then despite any losses to the minority, a Consequentialist defines the choice as ethical. The earlier pHarmX story in this book about the mass marketing of a proprietary aldehyde drug demonstrated consequentialist thinking. In that case, the few injured pedestrians and innocent car occupants hurt or killed by the drug's users were the means, and greater profit from a drug for the masses are the ends.

Making money isn't bad or wrong—it's very praiseworthy. What better outcome is there than a planet whose inhabitants are all wealthy? The ethical questions are concerned with how you make that money and what you do with it.

Cigarette manufacturers, banned in 1970 from advertising on U.S. mass media, shifted their sales to international markets. For those who travel, you may have noticed the dramatic increase in smoking in overseas markets over the last decades.

The ethics of producing and selling a lethal product here or abroad are the same. The difference is that other countries have laxer public health laws, decreased protections and lower consumer awareness of smoking risks. Once we in the U.S. gained a knowledge about the true effects of smoking and discovered the research these companies had conducted behind our backs for decades, they could no longer market to our ignorance. So, they went to places in the world where marketing to the uninformed was still possible. Interesting ethic. Very consequentialist.

So much for the universal right to life. As people in these nations grow more educated about the ill effects of smoking, they will also eventually turn the tide and oust these products. You can bet that ignorance is disappearing with each exhale.

[Just for a reality check, you may wish to visit the anti-smoking campaign videos starting with the 2007 Superbowl commercial from Shards 'o Glass Freezepops on YouTube. It's an interesting and poignant parody. It may also lead you to ask questions about government-sponsored court cases against these cigarette manufacturers while, that same government pays millions of dollars in subsidies to tobacco farmers. This is consequentialism to the nth degree.]

To finish up on this Ism, here are examples of how a Consequentialist might justify his or her choices about keeping or giving back those extra grade points.

### Consequentialism and the Unearned Grade Points

As a Consequentialist, what do you do when you discover you received more points than you deserved because of the teacher's math error scoring the exam? (The *Grade A Conundrum,* part 3)

- Do Nothing—think how happy family, friends and even co-workers will be with the news of my stellar GPA and the ensuing educational and professional opportunities. This is good for a lot of people and me.
- Do Nothing—this isn't going to hurt anyone. If I can get a scholarship based on this inflated grade, I save on student loans and the extra money can be spent on family's needs. The greater good is well served.

- Do Nothing—if the teacher knows, he may correct this error and go back and review everyone else's tests. That could hurt others if he made the same mistake on their exams. I stay quiet and those folks will be better off too.
- Do Nothing—I don't want to embarrass the teacher. He might even get into trouble. Apart from his questionable math skills, he's a good teacher, so the greater good is served if he keeps his job and lives to teach another day.
- Inform the Teacher—if anyone accidently discovers my secret, this is a slippery slope many others might rush down. I don't want that!
- Inform the teacher—if he knows about his error it will help him to ensure the rest of his students now and in the future will get the grades they actually earned. They also won't have to face this difficult and unfair choice.
- Inform the Teacher—I can help ensure that the school maintains its stellar reputation and grading standards. Adding myself to a world of cheaters would eventually mean no one knows how to differentiate between real scores and false ones.
- Inform the teacher—my teammates may suffer even as I earn a good grade, especially if the grading curve for the whole class brings everyone's averages down.*

  *There is an interesting ethics discussion to be had about grading curves, but we'll leave that for another day.*

## Virtuism and Universalism

It seems important in this online world to note that ethical virtuism has nothing to do with virtual reality, virtual shopping, virtual meetings, virtual dating, etc. The root word in this moral perspective is *virtue*.

Virtue-based ethics come from the broad concept that the viability of our society is dependent upon the consistent exercise of our human virtues. Virtuists would argue that society only exists through our interconnectedness and interconnectedness only exists if we predictably exercise our virtues with one another.

The other ethical framework I partner with Virtuism is Universalism. This is the ethical framework that loyalty to and concern for others should be universally practiced without regard to their allegiances or ours. Virtue-based and universally-practiced ethics rely on all of us exercising consistent virtuous behaviors regardless of our own gains and losses or group affiliations (so much for Subjectivism and Relativism…).Virtuists and Universalists support the unfailing demonstration of love, empathy and compassion in ethical choices.

Unlike the previous three Isms, Virtuism and Universalism concentrate on the means—the actions—rather than the ends (the outcomes) to judge what is and is not ethical (so much for Consequentialism). For Virtuists and Universalists, ethical decisions and actions support human values and obligations to all life.

> *Ethics Principle No. 16: What is moral is not simply what is accepted, but what a person of good character understands is appropriate on a universal basis.*

## Virtuism and Universalism in Practice

In an article titled *"Objectivist Virtue Ethics,"* highlighting how virtues find expression in the business world, Dr. Edward W. Younkins, Professor of Accountancy and Business Administration at Wheeling Jesuit University in West Virginia, wrote, "Employees are energetic, productive workers who: (1) focus on reality; (2) think objectively, rationally, and logically in applying relevant knowledge; (3) ask clear, pertinent, insightful questions and listen carefully; (4) search for facts in their total context before judging and evaluating business situations; (5) use time efficiently and effectively; (6) organize their lives and work toward accomplishing worthwhile endeavors; and (7) set value-producing goals and strive to accomplish them." Younkins names at least a dozen different virtues for ethical workers including being energetic, productive, focused, objective, rational, efficient, effective, organized, value-producing and accomplished.

This may seem like a long list, but psychologists report that there may be over 1000 human virtues: that's a much longer list! With that in mind, a couple of questions arise: Are all virtues of equal importance or are there priority virtues? If there are priorities, are they universal or do they change from culture to culture, guild to guild and person to person?

For example, are magnanimity and perseverance as important as love or compassion? If they are not, and there are greater and lesser virtues, who sets the priorities? How are they codified and enforced and by whom? There are myriad questions about how virtuous behavior is defined and supported. This is one of the liabilities of thinking about ethical choices strictly as expressions of certain virtues.

I would argue that our virtues do not change from time to time or place to place. Expressions of love may be very different in other societies and across the ages but love as a virtue is the same in France, Russia, Japan, Vanuatu, Inner Mongolia, the U.S.—in short, anywhere on the planet. So too, love was a virtue in the Middle Ages, during the Renaissance, before and after the rise and fall of the Roman and Greek Empires, before, during and after the Cold War era and in the present. While its outward form changes, love, as a virtue, is love.

While boundless and timeless, perhaps the need for the expression of virtues in our ethics does change. One might argue for instance, that as our world gets smaller and our borders become more transparent, virtues such as empathy, compassion and patience gain importance.

Certainly, honesty, integrity and trustworthiness in our leaders are being called into question on an almost moment-by-moment basis.

This all leads to asking some critical questions regarding the usefulness of Virtuism and Universalism in making consistent ethical choices: For instance, can we create a universal list of virtues or are they only culturally or temporally relevant? And if there was an objective list of necessary virtues, how could these be identified and prioritized?

Let's bring Grace in to help us out here.

## Different Perspectives, Different Priorities

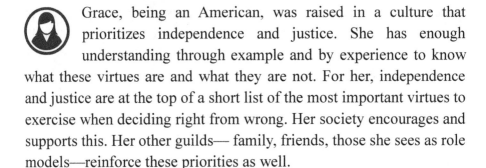 Grace, being an American, was raised in a culture that prioritizes independence and justice. She has enough understanding through example and by experience to know what these virtues are and what they are not. For her, independence and justice are at the top of a short list of the most important virtues to exercise when deciding right from wrong. Her society encourages and supports this. Her other guilds— family, friends, those she sees as role models—reinforce these priorities as well.

Grace's pen pals, Kasana from Kenya and Ivan Ivanovich from Russia, have their own lists of virtues created through their experiences and cultural norms. Kasana believes that kindness and charity are of utmost importance. Ivan Ivanovich believes the priority virtues are patience and diligence. Can they all make different ethical choices based on their priority virtues? Yes, by utilizing Virtuism and Universalism!

To illustrate this, I'll focus on a hypothetical scenario that occurs in all three countries. These may bring to light how different virtues drive different ethical choices. In this case, the choices will be made by their governments and media following fictional accidents.

Let us assume all three of these nations had recent nuclear power plant "episodes" that received completely different levels of media coverage. How did virtues drive their choices?

In the U.S., the moment news media knew of the nuclear accident, it viewed its task as generating continuous coverage of the responses of government officials, engineers, scientists, plant owners and builders, the local populations and aid organizations about all aspects of the incident. This was a 24/7 endeavor continued by multiple news outlets throughout the accident, its messy aftermath and its eventual clean-up. What was known and what was speculative were, for better or for worse, provided the same news coverage, especially through the early, live broadcasts. Some reported facts were completely erroneous. These errors were mostly divulged in later coverage. The government, attempting to stem any misinformation that might endanger the public, did its best to maintain control of the facts. In the end, this was seen by media and the public as government interference, accident mismanagement and a coordinated effort to minimize and misinform. After all, the U.S. public has the right to information for their independent choice-making.

Now, let us also assume the same type of nuclear accident occurred in Kenya. The Kenyan government, noting the lack of education and high illiteracy rates among many of the villagers residing near the accident site, took immediate and strict control of the media to minimize risks. Not only was accuracy a priority, but early, live news coverage would be missed by the villagers most at risk due to language barriers, lack of access to electronic media, lower levels of education and even sparse electricity. Therefore, the Kenyan government controlled the story, choosing to place government spokespeople and health experts into the at-risk villages before information was provided to the media. News outlets were kept away from the accident site for over a week. Only an official government spokesperson provided occasional, sketchy information to reporters and the public via short, irregularly scheduled press conferences commencing several days after the accident.

In the end, government control was seen by media and the public as interference and mismanagement due to the speculation it created among reporters faced with limited facts. Wanting to avoid widespread panic, the Kenyan government argued it had fulfilled its primary role in fathering its citizens—especially those marginalized people ignorant of the potential damages of such a complex disaster. The government did continuously request public charity for the displaced villagers who were eventually evacuated from their permanently contaminated homes and huts.

The third accident, in Russia, saw no national media coverage for a full three days following the incident there. International news, however, was ripe with speculations. The locals near the accident site were left to wonder, having heard explosions and alarms and witnessing plant workers being rushed offsite. Government, sworn to a duty of total centralized control to organize, coordinate and protect the country, brought scientists in to study the accident's severity and short-term consequences. Military units were also activated after two days for security and eventual clean up. All available attention and resources were devoted to fixing the problem. Information releases were considered a less-than-useful distraction from real needs.

It was also important to government leaders the country's global image be well managed. Government also prevented speculation and criticism by controlling the information flow from media outlets. Safety comes from supplying information useful to contain both the accident and people's reactions to it. In Russia, panic and misinformation are seen as the greatest potential injustices to the people.

In the end, while there were some accusations of the misuse of power, misinformation and mismanagement by government, these received limited coverage long after the incident in order to empower the public to move forward. People were expected to be patient and to persevere in the normality of their lives. Accurate information and long-term health concerns of dying victims dribbled out for years after the disaster, but these were never fully confirmed.

Okay, let's breathe in a bit here. Recall that these are fictional incidents meant to highlight the ethical impact of diverse virtues: independence and justice in the U.S., kindness and charity in Kenya, and patience and diligence in Russia. In these cases, virtues are being expressed in the ethical choices made about how best to inform, support and protect the public citizenry. Can we judge these actions strictly on the merit of the virtues exercised and if so, how do we do this? Can we believe, given the diversity of the groups being protected, that all of these virtues are applied equally and regardless of the make-up of different constituencies—educated suburbanites, illiterate villagers, community oriented socialists—as Universalism requires.

Were there other factors beyond their prioritized virtues that drove these countries' reactions? Absolutely. Perhaps they even overshadow the virtues highlighted here. But suffice it to say, as in all situations, our personal reactions to these different processes of ethical decision-making are based on our own understanding and prioritizing of different virtues.

## Other Challenges

The more emotion-laden the ethical issue, the more confusing the choice over the most virtuous stance to solve it. Consider, for example, the whirlwind of moral issues surrounding abortion, stem cell research and same-sex marriage, to name a few? To which virtues in our disagreements should we feel the most beholden? And do we prioritize virtues for the here and now, or practice virtues on behalf of the future?

Despite their seemingly universal appeal, the opponents of Virtuism and Universalism argue their weaknesses and inconsistencies. They also see Virtuism and Universalism untenable approaches to the ethical issues of today because they are nearly impossible to agree upon and implement globally.

• • • • • • • • • • • • • • • • • • • • • • • • • • • • • • • • • •

## INSTANT REPLAY

*The Isms at a Glance*

**Subjectivism**: me, myself and I define my ethics

**Relativism**: my family, group, or current situation define my ethics

**Consequentialism**: outcomes define my ethics

**Virtuism and Universalism**: our ethics come from virtuous behavior applied by all in all situations

• • • • • • • • • • • • • • • • • • • • • • • • • • • • • • • • • •

Let's look at some examples of how Virtuists or Universalists might justify their choices about keeping or giving back those extra grade points.

---

**Virtuism and Universalism and the Unearned Grade Points**

As a Virtuist or Universalist, what do you do when you discover you received more points than you deserved because of the teacher's math error scoring the exam? (The *Grade A Conundrum*, part 4)

• Do Nothing—the best expression of love here is loving myself with the good grade, loving the teacher by not fault-finding and helping those around me when I earn a better job that could allow me to be a better provider.

- Do Nothing—I have been persevering and devoted to my studies. My patience in quietly putting up with the inequities of past teachers', whose subjective grading may have unfairly harmed me, has finally paid off. With this teacher, I achieve grading parity. This is a just reward for my patience and good intentions.
- Do Nothing—I did nothing wrong here. I should accept this unexpected gift from the heavens with gratitude and move on to work diligently in my upcoming classes instead of dwelling on the past.
- Inform the Teacher—trustworthiness is based on honesty, two virtues which should animate our lives. After all, honesty is always the best policy.
- Inform the Teacher—I respect the rules of the school which prohibit cheating. This is cheating because some have been treated more fairly than others by this mistake.
- Inform the Teacher—I respect myself and I know about this error whether the teacher does or not. I have the courage to face the results of the truth.
- Inform the Teacher—there's no such thing as sort of honest. I must demonstrate respect for my peers and complete academic honesty.
- Inform the Teacher—after all, which is more important to the world, a better grade or my constant trustworthiness?

While virtues and their universal practice will animate a future universal ethic, their consistent practice is difficult in an inconsistent world. The next chapters will focus on a tool more useful in creating immediate ethical patterns of behavior.

# VARY THE PATTERN

*The Progression of Ethics*

*"A mile of highway will take you a mile.*
*A mile of runway will take you anywhere."*
—*Anonymous*

During my research on the difficulties with the Isms, it became increasingly clear that our ethics sorely needed re-assessment. Diving deeply into these traditional moral philosophies, I found them conflictive and often impotent in framing the right answers or even assisting us in asking the right questions about our ethical behaviors.

You can check any country's current news headlines for a demonstration that we need a new conversation about how to act ethically with one another. My work led me to two important insights. They wound up not only shaping my research, but also my life.

Here was my first lightning bolt: **As individuals, we must view ethics and our capacity to make right and wrong choices in the light of our ability to morally progress.** It is fruitless to think of our moral development as static and unchanging, as if the stationary grounding of the Isms could cover the boundless and ever-multiplying array of ethical situations and human conditions. A re-adjustment to our current, well-worn patterns is essential to making better ethical choices.

I have a rather lengthy but adventurous personal story about patterns. How a rather startling change to an established and well-mastered pattern probably saved my life . . . or at least my ego.

While I was in college, I successfully checked off a major bucket list item: I earned my private pilot's license. I had worked like a madman during my summers at a steel rolling mill in Seattle to earn college money and to pay for that license. It was a very proud day.

Much to my relief, flying seemed to come naturally to me. In fact, in a training regimen requiring a minimum of 35 flight hours, I earned my wings in just 37 logged hours. You can check my log book! My instructor, Brent Beck (great pilot's name, right?) actually referred to me around his offices as "SkyKing." But enough puffery; let's bring SkyKing and his ego back down to earth.

For any pilot, the first solo flight is a real thrill and one of the more nerve-racking adventures in our crowded skies. The place I trained was Boeing Field International (BFI) in Seattle. During my training, BFI was the 10th busiest, private and commercial jet airport in the U.S. It is still one of the main fields used by Boeing (the company) to test its new civilian and military aircraft.

After another routine hour of instruction with Captain Brent, we landed and taxied onto the tarmac. As I was just about to shut down the engine, he unbuckled, opened his door and shooting a glance at me, stated, "It's time. Take her up on your own, Skipper!" I gawked and blurted, "Are you sure? How do you know? I mean. . . it's only been a few hours since . . ."

*SkyKing circa 1980*

He interrupted, "Don't make me regret this, SkyKing. Get your butt in the air, you're wasting fuel!"

I faked a quick salute. As he shut the door, he leaned in and added, "Make sure you tell the Tower it's your first solo. They'll go easier on you." He winked, locked the door, and walked off.

In the whir of the idling propeller blade, I thought, "Okay, 'Mr. SkyKing,' it's time to buckle in extra tight and take this puppy up—and down. Real easy if you do it real easy!" I chuckled a bit as my mind was racing over all of the good habits I needed to remember and all of the bad habits I needed to avoid.

The plane was already in flight mode, so after a quick fuel gauge check, it was just a matter of contacting Ground Control, then the Tower and I'd be off for one circle of the airport then land safe, sound and celebratory.

It's worth mentioning that I was in my favorite Cessna 152, N4902F (November-Four-Niner-Zero-Two-Foxtrot). Favorite is about feel and control in this case, not design and color. It was a small, single engine, two-seater aircraft particularly good for beginners.

I'll shorten things a bit and just regale you with the basic radio communications between myself (02Fox) and Boeing Tower (BFI), as I was lining up on runway 14 Left to take off southbound for my first solo. The flight plan was to head south, turn to the left to stay in the air traffic pattern, turn left again heading north, fly the length of the runway and then turn left twice more, line up, descending and down— all gently of course.

These three legs around a runway are called the Downwind Leg, (as you parallel the runway), the Base Leg (as you turn just past the runway), and then the Final Leg (as you ease down toward a landing). Taxi home and done! But there's about to be a real wrinkle in my flight plan.

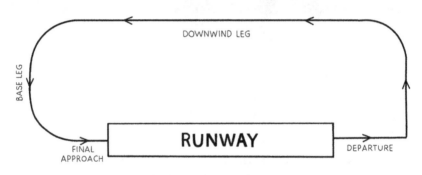

AIRFIELD FLIGHT TRAFFIC PATTERN

My radio squawks,

BFI: "02Foxtrot, hold short of runway One Four Left (14 Left) for landing traffic, a twin Beech on final." [The Tower is asking me to wait on the taxiway while a twin-engine Beechcraft airplane approaching the runway touches down and taxis out of my way.]

02F: "Roger, Tower, hold short 14 Left, 02Fox."

All Tower instructions are repeated back and the listening aircraft identifies itself to confirm the communication was heard and understood by the right plane.

After a few minutes the Beechcraft landed. A little extra time raises my nerves, but it also allows me a chance to think through each move one more time. Stay in the pattern. Communications should be short and to the point. Don't go above 800 feet. (Oh, most airport patterns are at 1000 feet above the runway, but Boeing Field is in the flight path of Seattle's major international airport, SeaTac. At BFI, the traffic pattern is restricted to 800 feet so we don't tangle with the big guys taking off and landing from there.) Finally, Flaps, Brakes, calls to Ground Control, and I'm in safe and sound!

My impeccable flight logic is interrupted by the radio once again. BFI: "Cessna 02Fox, taxi onto 14 Left. Cleared for takeoff." 02F: "Roger, Tower. Taxi onto 14 Left and cleared for takeoff, 02Fox." [Here was my chance. This was it! I'd only get to say the next sentence one time in my piloting career].

02F: "Boeing Tower, 02Fox providing pilot information. I wanted you to know this is my first solo flight." I probably should have left out the, "wanted you to know part," but I wanted them and every other pilot to know about my moment. I would later come to regret this.

BFI: "Roger 02Fox, we'll keep that in mind. Cleared for departure." [Did I hear a slight chuckle after that reply?]

02F: "Roger Tower, 02Fox cleared for takeoff for the pattern."

Throttle up. Engine sounds fine. Release brakes. Stay in the middle accelerating on the dashed runway lines and rotate up into the air after 67 mph. Easy peasy. As always, I'm in the pattern climbing to 800 feet. Flaps up. All is well. Feels like a dream. SkyKing has left the building!

I take my first left 90-degree turn eastward, then I'm up and over I-5, the busy Interstate highway paralleling the runway, turning left 90 degrees again and heading northward. I throttle back a bit. Safe in the pattern. All looks good. Time to radio in.

02F: "Boeing Tower. Cessna 02 Fox turning my downwind for runway 14 Left."

I'm headed home already. This will be a piece of cake!

BFI: "Roger 02 Fox. Continue downwind and await further instructions."

02F: "02Fox, downwind, awaiting instructions."

Wait.

Wait?

WAIT! Instructions? What kind of instructions? You don't get "further instructions" doing a simple loop in the airfield pattern for a quick landing.

Now my mind is racing. This has never happened in the dozens of takeoffs and landings with my instructor. What could they want to tell me? Have I done something wrong already? SkyKing is suddenly becoming SkyJerk or SkyMoron. I try to get back into the rhythm of my piloting, but this has definitely got me rattled.

About halfway through my downwind leg, where I should be preparing for my next 90-degree turn onto my Base Leg, the dreaded radio call comes through.

BFI: "Cessna 02Fox, take a short 360-degree right during your downwind and report over Veteran's. Reminder, altitude and speed restrictions around the hospital."

02F: [In my head: *"What the bleep did you just say????"*] Over the radio, "Roger Boeing Tower, 02Fox proceeding on right 360 and report over Veteran's."

I have no idea how I got that out. But like some thousand-hour experienced ace, I smoothly and briefly repeated back my instructions, even though I didn't have a clue what they meant.

My mind and heart racing, I start a right-hand circle out of the traditional, required landing pattern. I am going to have to ask the Tower for details before I really screw up. I understand a bit of what they instructed me to do—make a right-hand circle now; don't go too fast or too close to the Veterans' Hospital on the hill; and radio the Tower when I'm over that hospital. But why???? And should I stay at my 800-foot altitude or do I pull higher to fly over the hills looming ahead near the hospital, or stay here and watch the ground rising towards me? How close should I fly to this 16-story hospital building stuck way up into the air in front of me like the Great Wall of China? I'm not dazed, but I am confused.

So, with time *not* on my side, I somehow conjure up the following radio transmission:

02F: "Boeing Tower. Cessna 02Fox. Will you please repeat instructions regarding change in downwind pattern for 14 Left?" [Seconds now turn into minutes for me.]

BFI: "02Fox. Make a right, 360-degree right hand turn at your pattern altitude. Report back to the Tower when you are over the Veterans' Hospital. Re-enter the traffic pattern on your downwind leg at the end of your 360. An approaching 747 jet on final for runway 14 *Right* requires a delay for your clearance onto 14 Left." (Like many busy airports, BFI has two parallel runways, One Four Left and One Four Right.)

[I could not tell if I heard exasperation or patience in that Tower voice.]

02F: "Roger, 02 Fox. Right 360. Report Veterans. Thank you for the repeat, Tower."

No reply from the Tower. I can hear him on the same frequency talking the 747 down. I have truly lived up to SkyDummy while all the other listeners, including the distinguished 747 pilots, laugh at my infantile piloting skills and my baby-like confusion. Ah, well, I need to complete this blasted circle and get back into the pattern and land!

02F: "Boeing Tower, 02 Fox reporting Veterans." [Wow, that came up fast, as I glance at the top of the building towering to my left.]

BFI: "Roger 02 Fox, complete your turn and report re-entering downwind."

02F: "Complete turn. Report re-entering downwind, 02 Fox."

Another minute and I'll get back into the regular, predictable landing pattern. My 360-degree turn is going just fine. Altitude is still near 800 feet.

Wait . . .

A landing 747? A huge commercial jetliner landing on the runway next to mine? I remember very clearly during my instruction about "wake turbulence"! The bigger the jet, the slower it's moving, the more vortices flip off its wing tips. These little, invisible tornados of disturbed air radiate out along the plane's flight path, especially during landings and takeoffs. Wake turbulence can actually flip other big jets over if they mistakenly fly into its path.

What the heck am I going to do to avoid this invisible menace? Ah, shucks, just when I thought it was safe to go back into the pattern again. Whoops, speaking of which, I am coming back onto my downwind leg—better report.

02F: "Boeing Tower, Cessna 02 Fox re-entering downwind for approach to 14 Left."

[I can see the huge 747 flying towards me as it approaches the parallel runway. It's *ginormous!* The wake turbulence from this malignant monster must be reaching out to grasp every living thing within miles. My poor little plane and its poor little pilot, SkyButthead!]

The radio crackles again.

BFI: "Cessna 02 Fox. Extend downwind through South Bridge. Report turning Base for Final."

Holy Guacamole, now what??

02F: "02 Fox extending South bridge. Report turning onto Final." This one I think I've got. They want me to keep flying further than usual to extend my downwind leg to give the 747 more room to pass me and land. When I fly over the South Seattle Bridge, I am to report turning onto my Base and Final Legs as I head back toward the runway.

Good. *SkyThird-Cousin-to-the-Butler's-Helper-of-the-King*, almost on the way home again!

There's the bridge, time to turn and report.

02F: "Boeing Tower, 02 Fox reporting Base Leg onto Final for 14 Left."

BFI: "Roger 02 Fox. Cleared to land 14 Left. Caution Wake turbulence descending 747. Barometer 29.9. Winds 120 at 10 knots and gusting."

Oh, sweet-mother-of-pearl, that *wake turbulence*. Now the Tower is even warning me about this malicious, invisible monster patiently waiting to swat me and my ego straight to the ground. A few crazy barrel rolls and I plummet 800 feet and become a fixture on the bridge below me.

02F: "Roger. 02 Fox on Final. Cleared to land 14 Left. Roger, wake turbulence."

Well, no choice now. Wake monster or not I'm taking her in. I can see the 747-monster on the ground now lumbering toward its parking spot. You won't take me this time you silver, humped, jetted-devil.

No more distractions. I have to get back into my final approach. Flaps down. Speed slowed. Runway in sight. Altitude good. No, Houston-we-have-a-problem moment, here. This will be a great landing as long as I'm not flipped violently upside down with the aircraft shattered into four or five pieces. You know, just the usual concerns of a nascent pilot on his first solo flight. About 10 more seconds and I touch down out of this hell-world they call flying . . .

Actually, all of the rest of this landing went swimmingly. I touched down and got a hold of the Tower who told me to contact Ground Control for instructions to my parking spot, adding one final message:

BFI: "02 Fox. No choice on that approach. New pilot earned his wings today!"

02F: Proudly, SkyKing once again in complete control, answers, "Roger Tower, SkyKing shaken, but not stirred. Over and Out!"

No, not really. I came up with that response years after this incidence. It's what I wished I'd had the presence of mind to say. I more fittingly responded,

02F: "Roger Tower. Thank you! 02 Fox switching to ground frequency."

Unlike the flight, my answer was dull, but succinct.

If you stick to the rationalizations of the Isms, you will never land on solid moral ground. They are familiar patterns. But they can just as easily empower us to make poor choices as good choices, ethically speaking.

While using different frameworks implies different levels of moral reasoning, these old philosophies can be in agreement about a decision just as easily as they can be mutually exclusive to one another. We are unwittingly empowered by the Isms to rationalize both our ethical and unethical behaviors and to feel fine about them. The different responses in the *Grade A Conundrum* demonstrate this. Using all of the traditional perspectives, we see answers that range from unethical to ethical. We must change that pattern if we want to progress. We need a moral framework that allows us to see the degrees of selfishness or selflessness in our choices. Otherwise, our ethics will continue to waiver up and down the moral continuum dependent upon our individual motivations. We need a radical adjustment that, like the forced change to my flight pattern, puts us in line with the reality that all ethics should consistently tell us right from wrong independent from our motivations.

## Breaking Patterns

Let's bring Grace in again to illustrate the difficulties in our Ism-fixed patterns of ethical decision-making.

**The moral**: Moral progress requires conscious thought about our opportunities to make better choices, especially when we are wrestling with our conscience after a choice.

 **The scenario**: If you remember, Grace utilized subjectivism to make the choice between taking or giving back the bogus $20 change she got at the store. Under that Ism, whether she keeps the $20 for personal gain or gives the $20 back to avoid punishment, she feels good with the result. Let's amp up the good and bad outcomes of her thinking.

Suppose Grace's husband has announced recently he is running for City Council. Added to any personal outcomes about the $20, Grace begins to think consequentially about her ethical choices. She wonders if the best outcome here is one that helps more people. Certainly, an action that assists her husband's election fits that bill! He's best for the people in this role. Based on this reasoning, one of the benefits of giving the money back is avoiding bad publicity in case someone catches her theft. keeping it. The benefit of keeping the money for herself and her family (subjectivist thinking) is outweighed by the benefit to her community if she returns it (consequentialist thinking). In fact, returning the money to avoid bad publicity brings with it the possibility of good publicity. This could assist her husband's win to an even greater degree. So, she'll get the attention of the store manager and explain to her why she's bringing this back.

Interesting. If Grace were returning the money strictly as a Subjectivist avoiding punishment, she would be silent about that reasoning. She's not going to say, "Here's your $20 dollars back because I didn't want to get into trouble." Without commenting on a reason, the store could assume Grace gave them their money because it was the right thing to do. But as the Consequentialist, she can give the money back and with stated reasons and serve the greater good with the publicity.

Does Grace feel any sense of moral progress in all this reasoning? You bet! In her mind, she has gone from making a choice to serve herself, to a choice that serves her husband and the community. Is Grace making *actual* moral progress with this kind of thinking? Probably a small step. If she frames her choice only around her own outcomes, it's selfishly driven. If she frames her choice around benefits to others, she has at least taken a step toward selflessness. But she has still not progressed to the capital T-Truth that the money goes back to its owner because it's not hers to keep. That is the clearest ethical logic and highest moral outcome.

Jumping from one Ism to another, or even combining Isms, does not guarantee moral progress. After all, under that rubric, she would return the money even if it means bad publicity. The right thing to do has nothing to do with the outcomes to Grace, her husband or the election.

Grace's moral logic should, at a minimum, provide her with a universally-acceptable ethical action—giving the money back to its owner. At a maximum, her moral logic should provide her with a sense of progress toward her higher nature. Because they can easily work to justify all decisions, the traditional Isms contribute to a lack of moral progress.

Bottom line: beyond the other limitations of these Ism perspectives, they also do not account for or contribute to our moral progress. There is no final approach. There is no landing. We can repeat the same pattern or find no pattern at all. We never achieve progressively better and more consistently practiced ethical choices. We bounce unwittingly from Ism to Ism at our convenience.

> *Ethical Principle No 17: Moral frameworks and justifications that ignore the real victims of our unethical choices enable us to feel ethical while making the wrong choices.*

Moral progress is about increased recognition of our impacts on all effected stakeholders. That understanding is one way we move up the moral ladder.

So, let's break the pattern now with a few useful further instructions. SkyKing clear.

# THE FOURTH GRAIN: MORAL PROGRESSIVISM

### The Ladder of Ethics

*"We will embarrass our descendants just as*
*our ancestors embarrass us.*
*This is moral progress."*
—Sam Harris

Over my years of international consulting and education, I have spoken to people starved for a solid understanding of a good ethic. People want to know not just how to be right, but how to be *ethically* right. Effective training of any kind leads to understanding *and* action. Things that begin with words and end with words are meaningless. A good education begins with words and ends in deeds. This is certainly true of our conversations about where ethics should lead us. We want solid ground. We are parched for the trust we expect from ethical leaders. We are starved for the benefits on ours and others good choices.

For many years, I sought to determine why my research showed that people formally trained in the traditional Ism frameworks made worse moral choices than folks who had received no ethics training. As you've journeyed along with me through this book, we've discovered some answers to that question.

The Isms are taught as though they are all equally useful in justifying ethical choices, when in fact they are not. The traditional Isms keep the sea of words alive. That pond creates a sort of *laissez faire* attitude that any choice, no matter how wrong, comes from at least one moral perspective that makes it ethical. Granted, as I have noted before, we rarely, if ever, consciously label our decisions with an Ism. We make choices, and our current experience, training and education unconsciously help us rationalize them as correct. But shouldn't the primary purpose of ethics training be to empower us to choose ethically? As I have stated before, I wrote this book to highlight how our current education and training wittingly and unwittingly teach us that there is a right way to do the wrong thing—you just have to look at the wrong thing the right way! The Ism lenses help us do that.

People walk out of ethics classrooms, training rooms, board rooms, conference rooms and so on, empowered to make a choice and then consciously or unconsciously land on the framework that justify their choice as ethical.

Why aren't the Isms taught in a way that empowers only ethical decision-making?

Part of the answer is that we must first recognize and articulate the universal truths common to our individual and collective goodwill. Yet that process is fraught with a disregard fueled by the current environment in which it seems safer and more inclusive to assume that "everyone has the right to be right in their own way."

Since the Ism lenses preserve small t-truths, they support the perspective that every ethical choice is relative to who you are, what you know and what you prioritize—essentially what confirms (not overturns) our paradigms. Shifting those filters and heading towards capital T-Truth can be earth-shaking.

There was a March 2020 story in the *Guardian* about this. Certain members of the Ku Klux Klan, the white supremacy group, were casting aside their small t-truths of racial prejudice and inequality after being befriended by Daryl Davies, an African American blues musician. It seems improbable—maybe even impossible—but for the past thirty years, Mr. Davies has made it his mission to accompany over 200 Klansmen to a new, capital T-Truth about the races. Daryl reports that once his friendships take root, the Klansmen begin to suspect their old hates are misguided. [See articles in the *Guardian*, March 18, 2020 and more extensive content from 2017 at npr.org].

This is a remarkable story about individuals casting aside their deeply held beliefs and embarking on a journey of moral progress. It shook my own erroneous belief that these folks could never change. My bad! Healing can come in so many forms.

If we frame our ethical choices around moral progress, rather than becoming judgmental and exclusive, we become more circumspect and more careful in our consideration of others. This is the imperative in the words I stated earlier: ***Ethics are black and white, and we do have the capacity to morally progress past this moment toward a better one.*** The right question to ask is, how?

## My Second Lighthouse Moment

At the start of the last chapter I stated that I made two important discoveries in my research work. The first insight was that we must consider ethics from the perspective of our ability to progress morally. Here's the story about the second discovery.

In 2006, while speaking at a youth workshop in northern California, I was asked to give an impromptu business ethics presentation. On my timeline, I was still months away from successfully defending my dissertation research and earning my doctorate.

I was writing notes the evening before the workshop when I came across a framed quotation decorating the wall of my cabin. I believe in the mantra, "nothing by chance," so, for me, it was not mere coincidence that brought me to this moment. I read the quote on the wall and gasped. *Wait a minute. Let me read that again.* This quote by a Middle Eastern sage, the son of the founder of the Bahá'í Faith, spoken back in the late 1800s, encapsulated in one short paragraph everything I had been working towards in my six years of Ph.D. work. It read:

> *"Every imperfect soul is self-centered and thinketh only of his own good. But as his thoughts expand a little he will begin to think of the welfare and comfort of his family. If his ideas still more widen, his concern will be the felicity of his fellow citizens; and if still they widen, he will be thinking of the glory of his land and of his race. But when ideas and views reach the utmost degree of expansion and attain the stage of perfection, then will he be interested in the exaltation of humankind. He will then be the well-wisher of all men and the seeker of the wealth and prosperity of all lands. This is indicative of perfection."*[2]

Eureka! That was it!! Through the looking glass, I fell. My paradigm shift shifted. As a budding ethicist, business consultant, college professor, father, husband and friend, this quote is foundational to the reasons I can act for myself or act for the world.

This spiritual basis for our progress was solid evidence for me that my research findings weren't off-base or accidental. I had been looking for

---

2    *Selections from the Writings of Abdu'l-Bahá,* p. 69

a more effective tool for making good ethical choices and I had found it. This quote succinctly framed for me the steps up the moral ladder.

This moment was the seed for what I came to label in my research as the next ethical framework, the next generation of Ism, Moral Progressivism™. I would later define this new Ism as the capacity to make ethical decisions from an ever-advancing, virtue-driven set of humane values guided by our moral development and chosen through an exercise of our higher nature, free-will.

It's a mouthful, but this understanding became the backbone of my doctorate and my ethics consulting and teaching work around the globe. And it was the prime spark for this book.

> *Ethical Principle No. 18: We have the capacity to make ethical choices from an ever-advancing, virtue-drive set of humane values guided by our moral development and chosen through an exercise of our higher nature-driven, free will.*

Maybe it's best to examine this gobbledygook of ethics-speak beginning with a personal story about what we can know about the impacts of our choices.

## Ripples in the Pond

As you read in the first chapter, I had a real "come to ethics" moment when we were forced to close down our company, *Cravings*. I'm not referring to the steep learning curve under the shadow of the unethical practices of our sandwich-loving, unethical competitor. I'm talking about one of those life-changing experiences that come at you like a car running a stop light.

The day we let our 35 employees go and shut down our operations, we had an evening shift's worth of prepared food sitting in our walk-in refrigerator. It was all packaged and ready for delivery. Things had been prepared overnight, because it was our policy not to deliver anything older than 24-hours fresh. The food was prepared because of you stop the cooks at night, you've announced to the whole company, *"No deliveries tomorrow, we're closing down."* It was an expensive but ethical decision to keep things rolling along until we could drive up to the kitchen and talk to everyone the next morning. We had ourselves been given the shut-down ultimatum just 12 hours earlier.

We were close to our associates, so Glenn, John and I drove up to our operation in Bellingham. Our plan was to make the announcement, assist any employees who required special arrangements and support others in any way they asked. This was the least we could do for a loyal group of folks who had stuck with us over three turbulent years.

After giving them the bad news and answering everyone's questions, we gave out as much free food as our employees would take. Still, there was plenty left for deliveries that night. After the last farewell, the three of us from "corporate" decided to finish the deliveries ourselves and offer our customers a buy-one-get-one-free deal as a last hurrah. Our original plan had been to take all the food, frozen and fresh, to the local food banks. But our usual weekly delivery to them had just been completed a day earlier, so the food banks turned us down.

Since there were three employee positions required for our deliveries, one of us took over the phones, one manned the kitchen and I took over driving and deliveries. This is how the scales came to fall from my eyes. While I had been on deliveries numerous times over the years to talk with our customers, I had never flown solo. I donned my pressed, white coveralls, clipped on my purple bow tie (one of the five pastel colors that was supposedly the big-tip tie) and proceeded to my van. With a quick radio check, I drove off to my first address.

The first few of dinner deliveries went as planned. Folks were happy to see the meals but saddened to hear about our demise. Then, I got directions to a small house in a denser urban neighborhood on the north side of town. When I got there, I bagged the heated food, threw in the napkins, forks and knives, and headed for the front door. The answer to my knock was almost immediate. Not only were these folks hungry, but none of the three little girls and one little boy crowded around that door could have been older than ten. I began to swap my meals for a $20 bill wadded up in the hand of the eldest brother and asked them how they were doing. All four shouted, "Great!" Two of them added, "Hungry!"

I asked them how they liked our food, adding that I was one of the owners and always wanted to make sure people were happy, especially kids. The little boy said that they got *Cravings* almost every day when their mother was doing night-time work at the plant. That was a bit surprising but explained why there were no adults around for the delivery. By plant, he was referring to the nearby Alcoa smelter—one tough job.

He asked if I was going to be delivering food tomorrow, because they were ordering *Cravings* again. With a lump in my throat, I told him no more deliveries. We had to close our kitchen because of some trouble. If I could only show you a picture of the long sadness that appeared across his face. My heart broke. He didn't say anything, he just looked down. I told him that all of us felt sad too and asked what food he would miss most. I expected him to talk about the warm, chocolate chip cookies, or hot fudge sundae or make-your-own burger, but his answer was a shock.

"I don't know what we'll do," he said quietly, tears welling up in his brown eyes. When I asked him what he meant, he told me that whenever his mom had to do night work, she left him in charge of his younger sisters. Mom gave him $20 each night with the exhortation they could eat anything they wanted, as long as it was from *Cravings*, adding that the delivery person would be there to check up on them when he brought the food.

BAM! OUCH!!

Wow, I had never really thought about that aspect of our service before. This single mom knew that her kids would receive three important things from us each time she had to work the graveyard shift. Her four children would be getting a variety of healthy foods; that they would arrive hot and ready-to-eat so the little ones didn't have to cook; and finally, one of our drivers would be surreptitiously checking in on them during the nightly delivery.

This little guy was right. With us gone, what would they do? I told him to wait a moment and ran back to the delivery van. I bagged another four dinners with desserts and quickly returned to the door. He was waiting, nose pressed against the glass. I told him they should not eat any of this cold food tonight. But because we couldn't deliver the next night, if he put these bags in the refrigerator his mom could read the microwave directions and heat them up for tomorrow night's dinner before she left. With a big smile, he ran off to show-and-tell the food to his sisters and the door swung shut.

I walked away from that house with tears in my eyes for all we had lost. The sadness of the whole day really struck me then. I would ponder that delivery for years. What would this mother do now? And think about what we could have offered all the parents, single moms and dads, older sisters and brothers of kids left at home by choice or otherwise if we had stayed in business and expanded across the country.

But my tale of that night is not over.

As I have said before, nothing by chance, the very next—and what turned out to be last—*Cravings* delivery, was even more of an ethics-quake.

When I stepped back into the van, I got directions to a small basement apartment a few miles away. It was about 9:00 p.m., so I figured the dinner rush was probably over. Besides that, with all of our free food handouts, everything was just about gone.

I had a bit of trouble finding the place, but eventually arrived, bagged the food and accoutrements, then slouched towards the door, the previous delivery still weighing on me. I rang the buzzer and after a few seconds, a woman in her mid-forties appeared. She was obviously a regular customer so, recognizing my delivery uniform, she asked me to come in and help her unpack the hot food. This seemed a bit strange to me, since the process of unbagging a few microwavable packages, containers of cinnamon rolls, cheesecake, and napkins was not like building IKEA furniture.

As I walked down the narrow hallway and turned the corner, I saw the reason she wanted assistance. In the middle of the living room was a hospital bed, with IVs and monitors. Lying on her side was a small woman in her early thirties. She was not in any obvious pain, but it was clear that she lived in this bed in this apartment and required a lot of assistance. She could speak, but it was difficult to understand her and tough for her to control her movements. She was smiling ear-to-ear. I smiled ear-to-ear back, said hello, and added that I was her *Cravings* delivery guy tonight. She smiled wider, and her sister, walking toward the adjoining kitchen, asked if I would just set their meals on the two trays near the bed while she could get a straw and a glass. No problem. As I was doing this, I asked the sisters what they liked best about us.

The sweet young woman in the bed stammered that she liked the ice cream and cookies, but also liked the delivery men. I definitely blushed at that one. Then her sister added from the kitchen that the *Cravings* deliverers were always so kind to come in and visit them for a minute or two. It was the only time they had visitors. She also winked and added that they ordered three or four times a week since our female drivers delivered sometimes, and these gals wanted to talk with the male deliverers. She jokingly winked and told me this was the only time her sister got to meet eligible guys! I must have been three shades of red by then—happily married, but still red!

I had already brought in extra bags of food so I wouldn't have to go running back to the van. So, there was no getting around it, I had to let them know the truth about us. I muttered something about it being such a treat to meet them and wishing I'd done a lot more deliveries. I told them I was the president of the company and said I had extra food for their next few nights. I also added that, while that was the good news, I also had some bad news that had been hard on all of us that day. With that, I told them *Cravings* was closing for good and that they were actually the very last, but very best, customers we'd had our entire three years.

Like the previous delivery to the four kids, the older sister blurted out, "Oh boy . . . now what are we going to do?" Her younger sister moaned out a forlorn, "Nooo!"

I told them we'd had some trouble with an unfair competitor and our plans to open stores in other places had been axed. That meant we had to close here as well. By then, they both had tears. As shut-ins, this was their contact with the world and part of their daily joy. The elder sister went on to tell me how *Cravings* had been like a miracle for the two of them. Her sister was house-ridden and she herself was afraid to go out much and leave her alone. She just did the shopping and took care of her sister. That was their lives. Their parents had left years earlier to parts unknown. The visits from our drivers and our great food were the best things that had happened to them.

 Suffice it to say, while I offered apologies and words of consolation, what was left of my heart was now in tinier pieces. About all I could tangibly do was offer them the remaining food in the van if they wanted it for later. They accepted everything, even consoling me a bit, and then I dragged myself back to the van a final time to drive empty shelves back to the store.

I pondered these last two deliveries for many years. They had been beneficial in that I saw what we really had offered people with this brand-new idea. For some, it was far more than food delivery. These stops were also very challenging because, for me, they epitomized how we seldom know who our choices impact or how deeply they are affected. We had no say in shutting down our company—the investors/owners did that. But I truly felt for these people who had relied on us in ways that I had never considered.

In this same way, none of my ethical choices are just about me either. And rarely are my outcomes limited to just a few. My decisions have a ripple effect, the sum and distribution of which I may never know. Our unethical competitors who stole our idea for selfish profit had no inkling that their decisions would affect a single mom, four hungry children, two lonely shut-ins and I'm sure, many, many others in Bellingham, Washington.

My work as a consultant and educator falls into the same category. I will never know my effect, good or bad, on the thousands of my participants, students, their families, their co-workers, their communities or, if it ripples out far enough, our global village. My ethical choices fit the same pattern; I can't begin to know the extent of their impact.

It was Martin Luther King, Jr. who said, *"It really boils down to this: that all life is interrelated. We are all caught in an inescapable network of mutuality, tied into a single garment of destiny. Whatever affects one, affects all indirectly."*

## The Gravity of Our Situation

Perhaps another way to look at this idea of moral progression is by comparing it to the progress we make when we recognize and master increasingly complex ideas.

Let's take a simple but powerful example from natural law—how advances in our understanding of the force of gravity affected our abilities to perceive our world and enhance our capacities.

While early humans didn't understand it, they knew the reality of gravity well: they fell down, rocks fell down, cave-babies fell down, *all* things fall. This is one important and immutable physical law. We all fall down. But while our ancestors unwittingly experienced gravity, they could not wittingly comprehend it. They did not have that capacity.

An actual scientific look at gravity would not happen for tens of thousands of years until Aristotle. He conjectured that all objects move toward their "natural place." Remember, in his time everything was composed of some combination of only four elements: earth, air, fire and water. So, since almost everything had some earth in it, nearly everything moved towards it's "natural place," the Earth's center. We humans fell because, being partially made of earth, we were pulled toward the ground.

Interesting, if erroneous observation, but in Aristotle's model of the universe, the center of the earth was the center for everything that existed. Gravity worked as the force pulling everything toward it. This is called the Geocentric (Earth-Centered) Model of the universe, in case you're interested.

Now, this mistaken understanding of the law of gravity ruled us for almost 2000 years until Galileo Galilei noticed something important. No matter how heavy an object, it falls at the same speed as a lighter one. By experimentation, big rocks fell at the same speed as little rocks. Aristotle's law had said the heavier the object, the faster it is pulled down toward its natural place. In other words, in Aristotle's universe, big rocks must fall faster than small rocks. Galileo proved this to be an irrelevant, small t-truth in a remarkable way. He hypothesized that if a small rock falls slower than a large rock, if you tie the two rocks together, the slower falling small rock should hold back the faster falling large rock. But Galileo also knew that Aristotle's laws said a heavier object falls faster than a lighter one. Galileo was perplexed. He knew the total weight of both rocks tied together would be heavier and therefore they should fall faster. But he also knew, the slower, small rock should retard the speed of the big rock. But the combined rocks can't go faster and slower at the same time.

This was a glaring contradiction in Aristotle's Law and no capital T-Truth contradicts itself. Something was amiss. So, Galileo mimicked falling rocks by using wooden balls, some large, some small, some alone and some attached together. The result: they all fell at the same speed. Gravity was different than the rules Aristotle had presided over for 2000 years. Size and weight make no difference to gravity. Big things and little things fall at the same rate.

But wait, as Galileo also looked up at the stars, he noted they did not circle the center of Earth as Aristotle hypothesized. All the planets, including the earth, were clearly circling the sun! Galileo's conclusion, much to the unhappiness of the Aristotle-loving, Church scholars of the day, was that the earth was not at the center of the universe, nor was it even the center of our own solar system—the sun was. Thus, the Heliocentric (Sun-Centered) Model of our universe was born. And gravity, besides holding us to the ground, was somehow a part of the motion of things circling the sun.

As it turned out, while this was closer to the law of gravity, it was still not exactly accurate. After about 100 years of this Galilean truth, Sir Isaac Newton, struck by a falling apple in the 1600s, devoted the rest of his fruit-injured life to applying mathematics to gravity. Without getting too technical, to study gravity, Newton studied the planets as they "fell" around each other in what he described as an orbit. (Note that it was also Sir Isaac who said, "Gravity explains the motions of the planets, but it cannot explain who puts the planets in motion.")

Perhaps it seems hard to think of an orbit, or "falling around" as the same thing as "falling down." But this edict of gravity is actually how we launch a rocket into orbit. The rocket gets high enough and fast enough to continue falling down around the earth until we slow it sufficiently to fall out of orbit and down toward the ground.

Was that it? Did Newton finally define the capital T-Truth of gravity? Nope. We all know who showed up in the early 1900s to turn Sir Isaac's world upside down: Albert Einstein. Not satisfied with Newton's views on why masses attract each other with gravity, Einstein's general theory of relativity expressed through mathematics the nearly incomprehensible concept that gravity is the movement of objects following their shortest path which is curved by the spacetime warping effect of massive objects such as planets, suns and black holes. It's a bit like spacetime-potholes on a flat road deflecting a car.

Okay, that's far beyond my own, gravity-know-it-all capacities and way beyond the scope of an ethics book. Still, it may interest you to know that before I wrote this chapter, Einstein's mathematical theory was proven correct when shocked astronomers observed the surprise collision of two very dense neutron stars that sent out what Einstein had predicted: ripples of gravity. Like a rock thrown into a pond, these gravity ripples were detected with sensitive instruments here on Earth. (The Laser Interferometer Gravitational-Wave Observatory or LIGO).

Capital T-Truth? It may very well be. We are increasingly understanding more about the laws of gravity, including quantum mechanics, dark matter and dark energy, but I'll wait for the Star Trek future to explain it in their ethics books. [By the way, if you're really getting into this, there is a useful video titled "The Origins of Gravity" on YouTube.]

## Ripples Become Waves

This seeming meander into our changing truths about gravity is meant to be a physical example of how our growing capacity to understand something, anything, shifts our knowledge about our own natures and about nature itself. Literally, our "truth" changes with what we know and what we know changes with our increasing capacities to know it.

Following Einstein back to Newton back to Galileo back to Aristotle is not a tale of dumb, dumber and dumbest. It's an accurate portrayal of how mankind's capacities to understand natural laws advance over time. As they do, so too we are able to see our universe—and our place in it—in more comprehensive ways.

Even the immutable laws of gravity must be set aside in order to discover and master other 'impossible' capacities. If we stick to the law of gravity, we never take flight. Aerodynamic laws rule the sky. Balloons to gliders to powered planes, we progressed beyond the restrictions of gravity and mastered flying. Beyond certain technologies of the time, our lack of knowledge about aerodynamics is the most significant reason we didn't fly 200 or 500 or 1000 years ago. As I've pointed out, progress is made as we give up one paradigm for the next.

Do the laws of gravity disappear with the laws of aerodynamics? No, in fact, when we don't master aerodynamics well, gravity takes right back over and down we fall. Natural laws operate 24/7.

This transcendent journey isn't over yet. As we rocket into space, we must give up the laws of gravity and aerodynamics and master the laws of celestial mechanics. Gravity and aerodynamics are still in place but making this remarkable transformation from the limitations of falling down to the near infinite discoveries in zooming up requires our progressive development.

## Needs and Outcomes for Moral Progress

This analogy about science, technology and rational progress is, for me, a useful way to think about the needs and the outcomes of new laws for our moral progress. The old Isms will still shape our moral perspectives. But unless we investigate and utilize a new frame of reference aligned with the greater diversities of a growing global community, we are bounded to the restrictions of our past ethical choice-making. As I look at the world, I'm sure we don't want to do that.

In his book, *Business Ethics: Cases and Concepts*, Manuel Velasquez makes the following insightful observation: "A person's ability to use and critically evaluate his or her moral standards develops in the course of a person's life. Just as there are identifiable stages of growth in physical development, so the ability to make moral judgments also develops in identifiable stages." This is a profound comment on the progressive nature of the human spirit and the morality it molds.

We see pieces of this moral progression in all human activities. For instance, over a 100-year period, this nation went from a policy of unbridled resource-harvesting and over-pollution to the recognition of non-renewable resources and the need for sustainability and environmental preservation. One expression of this was the passage of strict environmental laws and our eventual progress toward attitudes of stewardship and sustainable development. While there are still nations caught in the old resource-wasting paradigms, the march of moral progress in environmental ethics is abundantly clear and advancing around the globe.

We see our moral progress through the evolution of other laws. I have several times pointed out the slow disintegration of our once solid rules concerning segregation and enabling discrimination and inequity. Where did those once sacred cows based on small t-truth go? We are moving past them as we switch our paradigms toward capital T-Truths.

We can and do morally progress and, from my perspective, we need a moral framework that defines and captures our ability to make that transformation.

Ethicists such as Bill Grace, Rushworth Kidder, Joseph Weiss, Rabindra Kanungo, Manuel Mendonca, and others argue that a universal ethic must include the fundamental understanding of our individual and collective moral progress. It is reassuring to discover that research among social scientists, organizational behaviorists and others highlight moral progress as the foundation of advancing our ethics. We cannot fly if we are bound to the Earth in old paradigms and dated perspectives.

So, let's climb the moral ladder and morally fly!

# CLIMB THE LADDER

*The Step-Wise of Ethics*

*"Even though the future seems far away,
it's actually beginning right now."*
—Mattie Stepanek

*"Those who stand for nothing fall for anything."*
—Alexander Hamilton

On Thursday, December 1, 1955, 42-year-old Rosa Parks, an African American seamstress, was on her way home by bus from a long day of work at a department store in Montgomery, Alabama. Segregation was supported by law at that time and, in Montgomery, the front section of public busses was reserved for white passengers, and the seats behind them for black passengers. When the white section was full, it was customary for the bus driver to ask a black person to give up a seat for a white rider.

At some point on the route, a white man boarded but could not find a seat in the "white" section. So, the driver ordered the patrons in the four seats of the first row of the "colored" section to stand, in effect adding another row to the "white" section. The three other passengers obeyed. Rosa Parks did not.

"People always say that I didn't give up my seat because I was tired," wrote Parks in her autobiography, "but that isn't true. I was not tired physically . . . no, the only tired I was, was tired of giving in."

Eventually, two police officers approached the stopped bus and after assessing the situation, took Rosa Parks into custody.

Rosa Parks broke the law. Yet most people today would agree that she did the "right" thing. By refusing to give up her seat to a white man on a Montgomery city bus that day in 1955, Parks initiated the civil rights movement in the United States. Over the next half-century, Parks became a nationally recognized symbol of dignity and strength in the struggle to end entrenched racial segregation.

## How Our Understanding of Morality Develops

Ending racial segregation in the United States is but one example of how morality develops both individually and collectively. But how exactly does this happen?

In examining the moral development that advances ethical behavior, it is useful to review the groundbreaking research of Dr. Lawrence Kohlberg, a child development specialist at Harvard's Center for Moral Education in the 1970s. His groundbreaking work is the heart of our cure for better ethical choice-making. Kohlberg's work is remarkably specific about the moral levels and stages through which individuals advance their knowledge, socialization, and moral awareness. Specifically, Kohlberg defines the human moralization process in three hierarchical levels, or steps. Each level has two specific and advancing stages of ethical awareness.

While these six stages are interesting, and I will refer to them occasionally for examples of decisions, the real meat here is this three-step model. Up the rungs of this simple ladder are the answer to our ethical vagaries. This climb dispels the foggy grey we have placed around the black and white of right and wrong choices. Of course, the ladder itself is not the answer. It is a tool useful in visualizing the steps upon which we stand to make our ethical choices. An understanding of these steps can provide anyone a remarkably clearer picture of his or her ethics. This ladder also allows us to examine the steps we don't choose in our choice-making.

The following is a summary of Dr. Kohlberg's version of that moral ladder. We'll adjust it some to fit it more closely with doing the right thing.

---

### Kohlberg's Six Stages of Moral Development

**Level 1: Pre-Conventional Morality—ethics motivated by anticipation of personal reward or punishment**

> **Stage One**: *Obedience and Punishment*—it is the immediate material consequences of an action that determines its relative goodness or badness
>
> **Stage Two**: *Individualism and Exchange*—people are valued only in terms of their utility. The right action consists of what we do to or for others who satisfy our own need(s).

**Level 2: Conventional Morality—ethics defined by the acceptance of the norms, rules and standards of our reference groups**

> **Stage Three:** *Interpersonal Conformity*—the individual acts to gain approval of others. Right behavior is conforming with the expectations of our family, peers, society or other groups.
>
> **Stage Four:** *Law and Order*—the individual respects formal rules, laws and authentic authority. Right behavior consists of maintaining social order for its own sake.

**Level 3: Post-Conventional Morality—ethical actions based upon virtuous and morally principled behaviors**

> **Stage Five:** *Social Contract and Individual Rights*—moral action is defined by the logical application of moral principles. Right tends to be defined in terms of both individual and stakeholder rights.
>
> **Stage Six:** *Universal Ethical Principles*—universal moral principles are based on the equity and worth of all human beings. Right means every individual is due conscientious consideration in all circumstances.

Before we go any further, I want to broaden our definition of moral development beyond simply maturing in our ethical behaviors. More specifically, I would define moral progress as **the broadening awareness of selflessness and personal detachment caused by our capacity to advance an intimate spiritual consciousness with others; that is, to see others through lenses of ever-increasing empathy, love and compassion.**

For our purposes, I'll boil Kohlberg's work down in the next diagram into the three distinct levels of the ladder I call Moral Progressivism. Each level is determined by the way we frame the means and ends of our actions.

---

## Moral Progressivism

**Level 1: "What happens to me?"**
Right or wrong is interpreted in personal terms of gaining reward or avoiding punishment.
(WHAT I THINK OF MY ACTION)

**Level 2: "What happens to some of us happens to me."**
Right or wrong is interpreted by whether we are accepted or rejected by the groups to which we belong or want to belong (our guilds). We follow and contribute to their norms, formal and informal rules, and laws.
(WHAT MY FAMILY, FRIENDS, AND GUILDS THINK OF MY ACTION)

**Level 3: "What happens to Us?"**
Right or wrong is interpreted by self-evaluated, virtue-driven moral principles based on truth and building trustworthiness.
(WHAT ALL AFFECTED STAKEHOLDERS THINK OF MY ACTION)

---

Put more simply, on the first rung of the moral ladder, Level 1, our ethical concerns are focused around the perspective, *"It's about me."* At the second rung, Level 2, our ethical concerns are focused around, *"It's about some of us."* And at the third and highest rung, Level 3, our ethical concerns are focused around, *"It's about all of us."* This is the ladder of our moral progress. Any ethical choice you make reflects at least one of these perspectives when you make it. It may not be easy to see, especially given our long experience with using the rationales of the other Isms, but when you made an ethical choice in the past, I assure you, you were standing on one of the three rungs of the moral ladder.

One caveat. It is easy to conceive of standing on a higher rung of the moral ladder than we actually are if we couch our choices in high moral level language. A glaring example would be a U.S. president justifying break-ins and burglaries or half-truths and lies to win an election. Fortunately acts of theft and dishonesty perpetrated at Level 1 or Level 2 (it's about me or about my colleagues maintaining power) are rationalized as moral through the higher ideal of maintaining a stronger, safer country under our exclusive leadership. These are words at Level 3 masking actions at Level 1 or 2.

In point of fact, a glaring problem with ethics today is sugar-coating lower level actions with higher-level words. Ethics Principle No. 5 covered this one: *Ethics are in the doing, not the talking!*

This ability to couch bad behaviors in words of good behavior is another one of the ways we come to believe there is a right way to do a wrong thing. There is not. If we are honest with our words, we will see the reality of our actions.

> *Ethics Principle No. 19: If we are honest with our words, we will see the truth of our actions.*

### The Steps of the Moral Ladder
Level 1: It's about me.
Level 2: It's about some of us.
Level 3: It's about all of us.

## Grace Climbs the Ladder

 With that, let's walk up the rungs of this three-step ladder and examine ethical choice-making. I'm going to invite Grace to participate and ask her this simple question as she reaches each step: Is it wrong to steal? Her answers will reflect the moral development achieved by mastering each step.

According to Kohlberg, at the first level of moral development (what he titled the *Pre-Conventional Stage*, or "before recognition of the law phase"), an individual is concerned with his or her own immediate interests with little understanding or acknowledgement of outside rules or laws. Ethical choices are framed here through the priorities of self-protection, self-aggrandizement and self-regard. The important questions here are, "What happens to me if I do or don't do this?" And, "What happens to the people who provide me something if I do or don't do this?" This is what Kohlberg meant in qualifying the first two stages of Level 1, Stage 1: *Obedience and Punishment* and Stage 2: *Individualism and Exchange*.

At Stage 1, ethical behaviors are those that increase our rewards and decrease our punishments. At Stage 2, we work to increase the reward for or decrease the harm to those who provide us something. Both stages are framed by the Level 1 question, "What will happen to me if I make this choice?"

"So, Grace, you are now standing solidly on the first step. Let me ask you, 'Is it wrong to steal?'"

"Yes and no", she replies, waffling a bit.

"What? Yes and no again just like the other Isms?" I exclaim. "Well," she posits, "at Level 1, stealing is wrong because I'm punished if I get caught. And stealing is okay if I don't get caught. It's also okay if I am stealing to help someone who helps me."

I get it. At both Stages of Level 1, right and wrong are framed by what happens to

Grace in making the choice. Grace doesn't acknowledge rules outside of herself except as means to gain reward or avoid punishment. For example, with Level 1 thinking, Grace might obey a speed limit sign, but only because she doesn't want a ticket if she gets caught. Like a child eating too many cookies, it's fine to keep devouring them as long as there's no punishment. Perhaps, even offering a cookie to the person who catches them eating too many may help avoid punishment. In fact, a person at Level 1 would define offering a cookie to avoid punishment as generosity. Fascinating!

Let's keep Grace on this first step and examine what she would do with that extra $20 change she got from the unfortunate store clerk a few chapters back.

At Level 1, she can justify keeping the money on the basis no one would ever know—she won't get into trouble. Or she will feel fine about keeping the $20 because it helps her with a tight family budget. Or she'll keep it to buy a birthday gift for a friend obligating him to reciprocate. At Level 1, Grace can justify keeping the $20 because the mistake was not hers. She's been short-changed other times in her life and this is finally karma (reward).

How about the opposite ethical action: Grace returning the money? At Level 1, she can justify this for fear the clerk might identify her or because she's been recorded on store security cameras. Or perhaps she returns it to ensure that her favorite clerk isn't fired for his incompetency. After all, he always gives her special discounts. Perhaps, she returns the money hoping for recognition for her "generosity"—that's a reward of sorts. Perhaps, she chooses to take it back, so she doesn't feel guilty. That's avoiding an emotional punishment.

Regardless of her final decision, as a Level 1 thinker, Grace has two completely opposite actions she can justify as ethical. And therein lies the problem with ethical decisions made from the first rung of the moral ladder. On this step, Grace has not yet progressed to a level of moral reasoning that considers her impact on others. Her moral behavior is driven only by self-reward or punishment avoidance.

Ethics are not ambiguous. Clearly, the ethical choice is to take the money back. But even though Grace *can* do the right thing at Level 1 by returning it, as you witness in her answers, this rung of the moral ladder does not always guarantee the right ethical choice.

By the way, you may have noticed Level 1 reasoning sounds very much like subjectivism. And you are correct. What's the difference? If you know all three steps of the ladder, then unlike subjectivism, Moral Progressivism urges you to consider not only where you stand in making a choice, but also provides a glimpse of what a choice at higher steps might look like. The moral ladder begs the question: What stopped you from choosing at a higher rung?

**In this sense, all of the traditional Isms are like snapshots showing our ethics at one moment in time—the moment of choice. Moral Progressivism is akin to a movie that can be rewound to review our actions or fast forwarded to look at different ethical results.**

Let's leave Grace hanging a moment and translate Level 1 thinking using business examples. Corporate fraud is justified at Level 1. So too, is employee theft. So are the lies and half-truths in false advertising or fraudulent product labeling. Look at the controversies over what can be marketed as an organic or green product as their sales increase. ENRON utilized Level 1 justifications in bending accounting rules and in their use of coded language. The reward for the business in all these examples is profit. I do not know if senior management at ENRON wanted to step up the moral ladder, but we can see in their illegal actions a demonstrated, rational capacity that could have taken them there.

One last thought about Level 1. As I stated earlier, if you see subjectivism in these rationalizations, you're correct. At lower levels of the moral ladder, the other Isms are quite potent.

Let us continue ascending these steps with Grace.

Moving up to Level 2, (what Kohlberg called the *Conventional Level* of moral thinking, as in "the recognition of conventions and rules"), an individual advances morally when he or she replaces an internally created set of self-serving rules (Level 1) with recognition and use of externally-generated rules that can bring benefits to others. Level 2 moral reasoning gives significant weight to making ethical choices that fall within norms, guidelines, rules and laws of the groups or guilds with which we are affiliated. Unlike Level 1 thinking, at Level 2, we finally recognize and learn to obey legitimate authority.

Grace is patiently waiting on the second step. So, I'll ask her that same simple question, "Grace, you're now a Level 2 thinker; is it wrong to steal?"

Again, Grace frustratingly replies, "Yes and no."

I'm a bit puzzled, so I ask, "How can you still get two answers? You've stepped up a moral rung, right?"

"Because, silly," she grins, "at Level 2, my answer depends on whom I listening to. If it's against the norms of people I care about or am connected to, then stealing is wrong. If they accept it as an okay practice, then stealing is fine."

"Ah," I answer cautiously, "this is the Stage 3 *Interpersonal Conformity* Kohlberg was talking about in Level 2, right?'

"That's a bit heavy, but you're right." replies Grace. "If the norms of my group say stealing is okay, I'll conform to those norms. If my group says stealing is wrong, I'll conform to *those* norms."

"What about the law?" I ask.

"Well, as you've already pointed out in Chapter 1, laws are just codified social arrangements. This is why Kohlberg called Stage 4, Level 2, the *Law and Order* Stage (I can hear Jerry Orbach, rest his soul, humming the theme song now). At Stage 4, stealing is wrong if it breaks the laws of society or violates some set of Divine Commandments. Laws are really just highly formalized norms of behavior. If there are no laws against it, stealing is okay."

Now, I am really puzzled. "Grace, where are there no laws against stealing?"

She's smirking again. "You've heard of bribery! This is acceptable behavior in many countries. Where do you think the money for the bribes comes from? It has to be quietly taken under the table. There's no business accounting category titled 'Bribes and Payoffs.' Bribe money always comes from somewhere hidden, like stockholders' pockets or past and future customers' wallets. The money for bribes has to come from someplace covert. That's basically stealing!"

"And so it is," I say with some resignation.

So, a person or company making payoffs is actually rationalizing stealing because there is no direct law against those bribes in some of the places they do business. Level 2 thinking can justify stealing as ethical or unethical depending upon whose laws you choose.

At Level 2, Grace's quandary about returning the $20 may have different ethical reasoning, but like Level 1, there are still two answers. For example, she can keep it if there's no store policy about giving it back. At Level 2, she can justify holding on to the money on the basis her family deserves what she can now purchase for them. She might keep it knowing her friends would think her crazy to return it, or if she is aware of friends who kept such ill-gotten booty in the past.

But at Level 2, Grace can also rationalize giving the $20 back. Even if she knows of no store policy, she may interpret keeping this money as stealing, and in this country, that's against the law. Perhaps her friends will think her dishonest and reject her if they find out she hasn't given it back. Maybe she returns it on the basis keeping it sets a bad example for her family, who might then think less of her.

Again, at Level 2, Grace is faced with ambiguous ethical solutions dependent upon the group she most wants to be connected with. In either case, "Yes, return the $20," or "No, keep the $20," the act of stealing is still being judged, not on its impact to the victim, but on Grace's acceptance or rejection by those with whom she is allied.

A business example of Level 2 thinking is seen in any company's offshore outsourcing of dangerous manufacturing jobs or environmentally damaging production processes to countries with more lax workplace laws or minimal environmental regulations. Bribery, unsafe working conditions, environmental damage and a host of other unethical offshore practices are justified at Level 2 since these practices are not violating foreign laws.

It is worthy to note that, at Level 2, following the law is done for the sake of obeying the rules. This is not recognition about whom the laws protect. The focus here is about not violating rules in order to avoid poor consequences. A higher level of moral motivation does not ignore the negative outcomes and rights of the victims that the laws are established to protect.

As with Level 1 thinking, we can see the heritage of the Isms at Level 2. As we know, both relativism and consequentialism judge ethical actions on the basis of group conformance and the benefits gained by the majority—the greater good.

## At Last, the Third Step

Finally, we have reached the top rung of the moral ladder, Level 3. This is the apex of moral reasoning. Kohlberg titled this Level, *Post-Conventional* or "beyond the rules." Perhaps another label would be the *Principled Level*. At the third level of moral reasoning, an individual has a clear and fully internalized understanding of morality. There is a strong connection between one's actions and their impacts on others. At Level 3, ethical choice emanates from a comprehensive, logically consistent and more universal application of our virtues. Consistent empathy, compassion and trustworthiness abound here.

At Level 3, individuals can make an ethical choice regardless of personal consequences and heedless of the external pressures so relevant at the lower steps. A person at this stage is focused on an inner voice balancing spiritual, emotional and rational capacities. The virtues of selflessness, love and empathy become driving forces behind all ethical choice-making.

At Level 3, when I ask Grace if stealing is wrong, she finally has one clear answer. "Yes!" And when I ask her why, she says emphatically,

"Stealing is wrong because it treats others differently than I would like to be treated and everyone deserves the same rights and respect."

Rosa Park's action in the early 1940s to retain her seat on the bus, despite the bus driver's order to vacate it, serves as an example of the direct application of Level 3 moral reasoning. While many might argue this action was wrong because it broke the law, (Level 2 thinking), Ms. Park's effectively chose a position of moral equity not because of, but in spite of the personal and legal consequences to her. The law was unjust because it sanctioned inequitable treatment. By her action, Ms. Parks demonstrated moral reasoning beyond her own personal gains or losses. She certainly knew well in the South of the 1950s what the personal consequences of this action would be. But by choosing a higher level of ethical motivation, she enlarged the civil rights conversation in the U.S. from its *Conventional Level*, focused on the norms and laws advocating prejudicial behaviors, to the *Principled Level*, advocating equity and universal human rights.

For an employee or business utilizing Level 3 reasoning, the ambiguities of the traditional ethical frameworks disappear. Decisions about the efficacy of fraud, theft, internationally practiced child labor, bribery, gifting, financial transparency, etc., become staggeringly clear. If an action does not create trust or enhance the trustworthiness and respect of our fellow humans, it is neither planned nor executed.

> *Ethics Principle No. 20: If our action will not create trust or enhance our trustworthiness or the respect of others, it is neither planned nor executed.*

What we practice on others is what we expect for ourselves. Our choices at this third level of moral progress consider all stakeholders. Level 3 thinking does not allow behaviors which impinge on the equity and rights due everyone. Individuals operating at this third level would give the $20 change back to the store. There is no debate. They understand that they, too, would want the money returned if it were rightfully theirs. The $20 never belonged to them. Level 3 makes that abundantly clear. No circumstance justifies theft of any kind from anyone.

"Whoa, wait a minute," you say. "You said no stealing ever? What if my family is starving and there is available food wasting away on my rich neighbor's front porch? Certainly, I can steal that food under those grave conditions?"

It's interesting we can grey up any situation to create the illusion of ethical behavior. But as I've said from the beginning, ethics are black and white; it's the situation that makes them seem grey. Fortunately for us, Moses did not come down off the mountain with the Ten Suggestions.

The Divine Laws of all religions tell us stealing is wrong. None of them say, "Stealing is wrong, but see Exceptions A through Z of this law footnoted below." No, by Commandment and the universal law of man, stealing is stealing is stealing and it is never the way we wish to be treated ourselves.

*Moses reveals the Ten Suggestions*

We can certainly justify stealing, especially under severe or mortal conditions. But the truth is, unless I have the permission of all of the stakeholders who own the food—those who have the right to control it—all justifications for taking it fall into the reasoning of Level 1 (I need to take care of me) or Level 2 (I need to take care of my family). At Level 3, I am forced to consider and consult with all stakeholders who suffer or benefit from my choice. This is the clarity of Moral Progressivism. On this step, you cannot couch lower level behaviors in higher level words. It may not always be easy to make consistent choices at Level 3. But that rung of decision-making prevents us from justifying ourselves as more moral than we actually are.

Now, I must admit, faced with my starving children and someone else's surplus food nearby, I could justify stealing. What Moral Progressivism correctly tells me is that even though I believe myself to be a moral giant for saving their lives by stealing, I stand at a lower step of the moral ladder to accomplish it. Stealing the food from the owner totally ignores any of her plans, needs or rights. Stealing the food for the benefit of me and mine is ignorant of the moral obligations I have to the food's owner who may intend, for instance, to feed twice as many of her starving children with it.

At Level 3 we cannot ignore the capital T-Truth that while my children may live by my theft, hers are less valuable to me. Levels 1 and 2 of this moral ladder, while supporting my ethical obligations to those I love, ignore a profound choice I make in stealing the food and disregarding those who I do not love, or whom I love "less" as part of the moral equation.

Now, before you toss this book across the room wondering, "How could moral progress mean sacrificing children's lives for property rights?," let me add a significant part of the ethical answer.

Sometimes the cost of making a choice on the top step, Level 3, is so high there is no viable alternative but taking a lower level action. In this case, the option of having my children perish in recognition that all moral laws are created equal, is indeed too much to ask. But being forced to save those in my immediate care, especially vulnerable children, does not excuse me from making an effort to change the system in which such a tragic choice is present. In other words, progress up the moral ladder means two things. We not only wrestle with the circumstances and ethical costs of our immediate choices, perhaps acting at Level 1 or 2 when Level 3 comes at horrific price, but we also explore the changes required to ensure Level 3 behavior is not this calamitous in the future.

In other words, at Level 3 we are also obligated to work on changing an inequitable system.

If you're still holding this book, let's explore these difficulties in the next short chapter. But first, one last look at how moral progress walks us up the ladder from lesser moral answers to greater moral answers in our rationalizing about those extra, unearned grade points.

## Moral Progressivism and the Unearned Grade Points

As a moral progressivist, what do you do when you discover you received more points than you deserved because of the teacher's math error grading your exam? (The *Grade A Conundrum*, part 4)

### A Walk Up the Moral Ladder

| Level/Stage | Action | Rationale |
|---|---|---|
| L1/S1 | Keep the points | Who's going to know; I won't be punished, just rewarded. |
| L1/S1 | Inform the teacher | Someone might know— meaning, I'm caught and punished. |
| L1/S2 | Keep the points | This isn't going to hurt anyone else. |
| L1/S2 | Inform the teacher | If I change the grading curve, my friend may get a B instead of an A and I could lose his friendship. |
| L2/S3 | Keep the points | My friends will say I'm crazy for giving these back—I'll lose their respect. |
| L2/S3 | Inform the teacher | My friends know me as honest. I want to keep their respect. |

| L2/S4 | Keep the points | The syllabus doesn't say anything about giving points back. I'll follow the published rules that I know. |
|---|---|---|
| L2/S4 | Inform the teacher | The syllabus specifically says to inform the teacher about unearned points. I'll follow the rules. |
| L3/S5 | Keep the points | Don't rock the boat. As an elected student leader in my school, my fellow students have already let me know they want me representing them at all costs. |
| L3/S5 | Inform the teacher | I would be treating myself differently than others, which is unfair to all. |
| L3/S6 | *Always inform the teacher* | *It's the right thing to do and supports trustworthiness and the integrity of our system of mastering knowledge. Everyone wins—even me!* |

# IT CAN' T BE THAT SIMPLE

## The Tasks of Progressive Ethics

*"Be the change you wish to see in the world."*
—*Ghandi*

In this brief chapter, I'd like to wrap up some important aspects of practicing Moral Progressivism. Based on the energy of discussions, there is probably no more controversial an idea posed during my presentations and trainings than the moral question that pits personal or family survival needs against the rationale of stealing food.

The very dramatic ethical scenario at the end of the last chapter raises a significant and important responsibility in utilizing Moral Progressivism. Unlike the other Isms, moral progress requires us to consider our present and our future actions. The best way to do this is by using systems thinking in our ethical relationships.

What is systems thinking, you might ask?

In the 1960s, a biologist by the tongue-twisting name of Ludwig von Bertalanffy, proposed that every individual component of a living organism must work to the benefit of the whole organism to ensure its own individual survival. Cells, tissues, organs, blood—all parts of our bodies—only thrive by working cooperatively and sharing our body's resources to keep us healthy. At times, tissues, organs and other individual parts of us even give up resources to guarantee the whole system's health.

For example, when your hands and feet get cold, this is a systems response—your limbs are automatically deprived of blood flow to ensure there is enough warmth for the vital organs in your core. This is not a conscious process. On the contrary, all of the components in our bodies work interdependently and automatically. Cancer, on the other hand, may work automatically, but it operates *independently*. It does not cooperate or share resources with the whole system. In fact, it takes what it needs to survive in the short term, eventually sabotaging the entire organism that keeps it alive. This is not a long term strategy for living well. Neither are unethical decisions in society that work only on behalf of individuals or guilds.

Ethical decisions are, by definition, supportive of others in the community. Unethical actions erode the connections and communities that help us ultimately thrive. The interactions of society, community, organization, family and other guilds thrive where individuals cooperate. That is, where they work on behalf of the whole system in which they live. This was labeled earlier as our two-fold, moral purpose.

Perhaps a short example will get us out of the academic-speak. Consider the current controversies around global climate change. International accords have been created about environmental stewardship. But from a systems perspective, unless we all act within these agreements, our environment can be sabotaged by just a very few rogue nations who operate on their own behalf. Pollution doesn't need a passport or visa to slip across our borders. And because our earth operates with a living systems dynamic, each nation has the capacity to contribute to or subtract from the whole planet's balance. Environmental degradation in one spot becomes degradation in other spots. Global climate change has been impacted this way.

Because moral standards determine our levels of cooperation and interdependence, ethical behaviors are the glue of the system we call society. Moral progress prioritizes what's needed to ensure not just our own survival, but also how we will contribute to all of society now and in the future. As our understanding of our increasing interdependence grows, so too we must consider our ethical actions in light of that whole system.

In the scenario of stealing food for survival, at the highest rung of the moral ladder we know we would never take the food. At that step, we are also responsible for questioning how such dire circumstances were ever created. How does a world working cooperatively and interdependently allow this kind, or any kind, of extreme disparity? At Level 3 there are no "haves" that control the destiny of the "have-nots," and no wealthy who deprive others in what is often erroneously viewed with a Win-Lose ethic. That is, given the paradigm that resources are always limited, in order for me to get my share, you must lose yours.

At Level 3, the ethical paradigm is Win-Win. Wanton desperation among some of us forced to steal for survival becomes the active concern of our fellow citizens. In a Level 3 world, there are safety nets that help protect us from disasters or even our own poor choices.

We see today's versions of these Level 3 safety nets now in the proliferation of food banks, homeless shelters, disaster relief agencies, non-governmental aid organizations, free health care clinics and so on. Most of these didn't exist 100 years ago. But in a Level 3 world, safety nets would eventually disappear. For example, food banks are great, but I'm sure we don't view the better future as one supporting more food banks. The better future is one that needs no food banks.

The norms of society are based on our conventions with one another. Selflessness may be a part of those norms in every society. Growing interdependencies that emerge as our national sovereignty fades and a global sovereignty emerges, require us to examine our interconnectedness. The 2020 global pandemic spotlights this interconnectedness and is the current acid test for global cooperation. Vulnerability to this disease is shared across the planet by all populations, age groups, economic and social classes, national sovereignties, education levels, political and religious proclivities, races, ethnicities and genders. Just like global warming and pollution, COVID-19 requires no passport, visa or citizenship card to cross borders and influence entire societies. Manmade boundaries and national sovereignties prove to be no inoculation from its affects. As a global people, we face this sickness together; we fight this sickness together; and we finish this sickness together.

Beyond vaccines, the cure for this universally shared virus is a universal inoculation effort. This pandemic also challenges us to create a global organization dedicated to staving off all future such emergencies. This glimpse at a required, unified front to beat all viruses is an occasion to celebrate our interdependence. Building strength in numbers, so to speak. My faith exhorts the idea that we are all leaves on the same tree and we must act accordingly. Therein lies the real cure!

Moral progress enables us to consider our impact on the whole. For the long-term survival of family, community, state, nation, and the world, systems thinking is the only answer to a universal morality. Moral progress is the only framework that enables us to consistently consider the equity and justness of the world community and the part each of us plays in it.

Big issues? Yes. Solvable immediately? Probably not. But they are solvable. Honest solutions will definitely involve our interdependencies and a systems morality. One person can make a difference, although it seems miniscule. Still, I am reminded of a quote by the famous American cultural anthropologist Margret Mead, *"Never doubt that a small group of thoughtful, committed citizens can change the world. Indeed, it is the only thing that ever has."*

No food banks? No homeless? No poor houses? Is this a utopian dream? There are remarkable trends in morality happening in our present world. While the disparity between the rich and the poor has never been greater, a holistic responsibility and connection is also emerging and growing. As one example, consider those rich enough among us to build their own "golden castles," close their gates behind them, and provide for every need or want they desire without any of the rest of us. They seem successfully independent. But they recognize the quality of their lives is being negatively impacted by a disparate and desperate world they view daily from their castle windows.

No one can live the richest life and not be impacted by the sight of disparity, starvation, disease, illiteracy, viral pandemics and all other global malignancies. The rich thrive best when those living outside their castle walls also thrive. We have witnessed this realization as wealthy individuals create charities and relief organizations and provide multi-million and multi-billion dollar donations to organizations such as the United Nations.

We cannot demand people work towards Level 3 moral thinking in systems that are currently operating at Levels 1 and 2. Sacrificing life to avoid stealing is an extreme, but plausible, example. Stealing to live is justifiable at Levels 1 and 2, but it is obviously not the permanent solution. It is a short-term answer to a much larger problem. With an awareness of moral progress, we the desperate food stealers and we the excess food owners are responsible for changing the system so we all thrive together. I am always marveling at the extreme scenarios I see in ethics books that incite conversations about such trade-offs. Do I save three lives by throwing this runaway train stop-switch or sacrifice one person by not throwing that switch? Do I steal an expensive drug the doctor refuses to give me so I can save my significant other or wait patiently as they wither away? Do I give up the hiding place of people being unjustly hunted or lie to the thugs seeking information about their location?

These are actual conundrums in numerous ethics books. My experience in these discussions is that no one, including the author, asks the two most important questions: *What needs to be done to ensure this scenario is never repeated? And who will do it?*

Let me provide a solid answer to both questions. We need to walk up the moral ladder, and one choice at a time, work together on a universal ethic. This also answers the second question. The who is us!

One final thought on "Us."

Barry Schwartz, psychologist and author of *Practical Wisdom*, spoke in a Google Talk recently. He told a story about individuals and their sense of responsibility to the society around them. In a survey of the Swiss, when asked if they would personally be willing to have a nuclear waste dump built in their community, 50 percent said yes. When another group was asked the same question but was told they would get an additional six weeks' worth of salary every year if they allowed it, only 25 percent said yes. The hypothetical situation posited with zero compensation had DOUBLE the amount of people who responded yes. Wow. Why? It turns out, when offering someone money to be socially responsible, you have implicitly introduced the idea that this action is a matter of self-interest, rather than a matter of society's health. And when it is framed as a matter of self-interest, it becomes self-evident that the building of a nuclear waste dump in their community is not in their self-interest, no matter what they are paid.

It seems that moral progress built through more systemic thinking may not be as hard as we think.

# TO INFINITY AND BEYOND!

### *Your Ethical Future*

*"How wonderful it is that nobody need wait a single moment before starting to improve the world."*

—*Anne Frank*

After the orbiting Hubble telescope had taken its breathtaking pictures of celestial phenomena across our universe, scientists thought to use it to answer an age-old question: How many stars are there?

They tasked this magnificent machine to take a time-lapse photograph of a specifically dark part of our skies. The thinking was that this darker region would have less stars and our count would provide a conservative estimate. You know scientists.

They pointed one of the telescope's cameras at an area of the night sky the size of a drinking straw and left the lens open for nearly five days. This allowed the dim light from distant stars to register, allowing a good count. The final picture was a shock. From this particularly dark patch of the universe, there were over 10,000 points of light! But even more astonishing, when these lights were examined, it was discovered they were not stars; they were galaxies. Imagine looking through a straw at the night sky and that tiny circle contains 10,000 GALAXIES! (By the way, that comes to a universal total of ten-trillion galaxies with one-septillion total (1,000,000,000,000,000,000,000,000) stars in the known universe—by conservative estimate.)

I think of that story and know with all of my being that our universe is full of more abundance than we could ever possibly imagine. The old thinking that someone has to give something up in order for us to gain something is such an enormous misperception. It haunts our past. It rules our lives. It creates false barriers that have held us back as individuals and as societies since there were individuals. It has informed the old Isms of our ethics.

The universe is full of abundance. Every time I sit down with folks who believe in scarcity, I am reminded we cannot possibly think we do not have enough. Oh, I understand that there are great disparities in how we divide that abundance among ourselves right now, but that itself is an outcome of this oft-perceived, paradigm of scarcity.

The first reaction I get from people feeling pushed by the idea of moral progress is that they are giving something up to think so much about others or the larger global village when they make choices. Some call it national sovereignty. Others think of it as losing their rights or their rightful opportunity for gain, even if it is at the expense of others. Businesspeople often say such thinking takes an organization away from its primary mission to profit and expand. Still others claim we all have to share the same religious or cultural beliefs in order to galvanize such a world. All of these comments are directly or indirectly about loss and scarcity.

Moral Progressivism is not a Win-Lose game. There is so much to go around, every one of us can believe in it and practice it. I am reminded of the two perspectives on rose bushes. There are those who look at a beautiful rose bush and ask, "Why does such a beautiful flower have to have so many thorns?" And there are those who look and say, "Isn't it wonderful that a thorn bush has so many beautiful roses!"

As I stated in the introduction, the real truth is that we have only two choices about climbing the moral ladder. We can stay on the lower rungs, believing in our current situational ethics and thinking that being treated fairly by others who demonstrate honesty and integrity is a luck of the draw. Or we can believe we have the capacity to create a world that operates on the same truths practiced by everyone for everyone. A world where ethical choices are those that build trust and trustworthiness. In which world do you want to live?

In the classic black and white movie, *The Oxbow Incident*, the character Gil Carter, played by a young Jimmy Stewart, is reading the letter of an innocent lynching victim. The focus is on our human compassion and oddly, very appropriate to this book. Gil Carter reads aloud, *"There can't be such a thing as civilization unless people have conscience. Because if people touch God anywhere, where is it except through their conscience? And what is anybody's conscience except a little piece of the conscience of all men who ever lived?"* With moral progress, we build our own conscience and connect it with others.

## The Most Important Human Virtue

If I were to ask you what the most important human virtue is, what would you say? In my experience, about 91 percent of us say it's love. That's a good answer.

Try this idea. I believe trustworthiness is actually the primary human virtue because trust is the foundation upon which all other human virtues rely. Think about it: without trustworthiness, true love is impossible. Without trustworthiness, compassion, empathy and forgiveness are impossible. Without trustworthiness, selflessness doesn't exist. Without trustworthiness, kindness, patience, humility, perseverance and diligence don't exist. There is a useful quote on an interfaith website about this:

> *"Truthfulness and trustworthiness involve much more than not telling lies; they embody the overarching capacity to discern, value and uphold truth itself. Without these spiritual qualities, neither individual nor social progress is possible. Justice is vital to the establishment of unity and harmony at all levels of society, as it provides the standard by which individual conduct and collective effort are judged. A requirement for living a life of service to humanity, then, is constant effort to develop truthfulness and trustworthiness, ensuring that they are ever-present in thought and action."*[3]

> ## *Ethics Principle No. 21: Ethics are based on an exercise of our virtues, not an exercise of our rights.*

All of the great faiths remind us we are born noble beings. The key to a life of trustworthiness is practicing that innate nobility with every choice you make. That is how we reclaim an ethical world one choice at a time. That is how we better ourselves as individuals. When we live ethically, the world becomes a better place. As the world advances ethically, we become better people. But what steps can we actually take to do that? In all the words and chapters and tomes written on this subject, are there actionable ways to morally progress? You bet!

Let me provide nine proven steps that march us up that moral ladder. I would recommend you start at least one of them immediately and pay attention to your outcomes. I call these the *Noble Nine*.

---

3   Soulfood.com.au

# The Noble Nine

### The First Noble Step: *Ladder Up!*

Research shows that awareness of our capacity for moral progress actually helps us make better choices. So, if you've read this book, it's too late—you have that awareness in spades now. While it may be a well-worn habit for us to rationalize and excuse to our Isms' content, you've already taken the first noble step in raising your own capacity to morally progress. That alone can make a difference to your ethical choices. Congratulations!

### The Second Noble Step: *Catch a Glimpse*

The tallest shadow is always cast from the top! We are all practiced on the steps of this moral ladder. We used them every time we made an ethical choice even if we weren't aware of them. You are now. If you're like me, you've climbed up sometimes and you've climbed down sometimes. Our moral progress comes in 'upping' more than we 'down'. Whether it's a one-step climb or a two-step climb, strive and imagine the view from the top. It is a great glimpse at the Noble Edge!

### The Third Noble Step: *Be Your Own Guru*

This wisdom is yours. Your decisions are yours. Every step up the moral ladder is yours. You are the only "guru" around when you make most choices. Make those choices wisely knowing every step up is well-supported. Try linking your views about right and wrong with your own personal progress. Exercise your best virtues. Know with absolute certainty that your climb comes with the moral assurance of every great spiritual tradition in human history. You cannot fail; you can only progress.

### The Fourth Noble Step: *Practice "Behindism"*

Leave the old Isms behind. Your actions, justifications, rationalizations and explanations should always be worthy of the trust of others. Concentrate on the question, "Is this action going to create more trust with others or erode it?" If it is the latter, you're probably justifying your ethical decision with one or more of the less than useful Isms. Rely instead on your sense of moral progress. Your insight can serve you well.

### The Fifth Noble Step: *Pass Around Your Decoder Ring*
Share your codes liberally. Let people know what you're saying and what you mean. Be forthright. Hiding behind words or the *real meaning* of your words is often a step downward. Whether you're asking a question or making a statement, be true in your intentions and authentic in your actions. Ask others, especially the stakeholders in your choices, for their input. Remember, ethics is a public process.

### The Sixth Noble Step: *Trustworthiness Is as Trustworthiness Does*
Your choices either enrich or impoverish your trustworthiness. A lifetime of building trust can be shattered in moments. On the other hand, opportunities from building trust are limitless and the climb toward better ethical decision-making is part of the purpose of our lives. Transformation is a challenging process but it is filled with life-changing possibilities. What goal in life doesn't require personal commitment? So, commit!

### The Seventh Noble Step: *You Are What You Eats*
Here are a few questions to ask yourself that personalize the ethics of your choices. I call these the *Ethical Acid Tests* or *EATs*.

- Does my decision stand up to public scrutiny? What if my actions were publicized on the front cover of tomorrow's *New York Times* or broadcast on Social Media, CNN, NPR or other prime time news?
- Do I want my partner, children, neighbors, co-workers, colleagues, boss or employees to do what I am about to do?
- Do I want this action to be on my permanent record, or added to our family rules or detailed in my organization's policies and procedures manual?
- Are the outcomes of my choice good for all stakeholders?
- Does this decision advance the long-term common good?

- Does this action create trust with others?

If your answer to *any* of these *EATs* is, "No," then don't do it!

## The Eighth Noble Step: *Don't React, Respond*

Ethical actions result from utilizing your *Knowledge, Judgment* and *Will.* Allow time for each of these capacities to coalesce when you are choosing. Start with what you know. Utilize judgement to ensure you're doing the right thing with what you know. Examine which step of the ladder you're using. Then, once satisfied, act! It's easier to make an enlightened ethical choice after some contemplation time. That also allows for those intangible "aha" moments that bring new patterns.

## The Ninth Noble Step: *Notice Your "Other-than-Yourself" Moments*

Acute awareness of "other-than-yourself-ness" is a distinct sign that moral progress is seeping into your choice-making. So does a growing reliance on selflessness. If the ethical tools and ideas in this book seep more and more into your ethical moments, you're well on the way to becoming a greater force of change for good.

## Conclusion

So, is that it? Are we finally done? Well, we are with this book maybe, but never with the process. No person ever crosses the moral finish line and ends his or her quest to be consistently virtuous. It is a lifelong journey to ever-advance on all three pillars of wisdom.

I journey with you. As an official ethics advocate, I continually caution my listeners and readers that my title does not mean I am somehow any more moral than anyone else, as long as they, like me, are striving to be better tomorrow than they are today. I step up and down the ladder all the time—less than I used to, but up and down nonetheless. I live in the same world as everyone else—tempted by subjectivist gain, immersed in blissful relativity and marinating in a focus on the gains while ignoring the means to get them.

If there is any difference, it is that I believe I have developed an incredibly useful way to think about my ethical choice-making. I have found that learning and thinking about moral progress has assisted me to make better decisions—not always and not consistently—but with increasing regularity. And that's where meaningfulness starts. That's where progress starts. That's the Noble Edge!

What you think about ethics becomes your ethic. If you believe ethics are grey, then you will find yourself in greyer and greyer situations where the choices get blurrier and blurrier. Where you see, know and act with the assurance that ethics are there to tell us right from wrong, so too, will you be put into more and more situations where the answer is obvious despite the complexity of the circumstances. It takes work and the top rung of the moral ladder can sometimes appear impossible to achieve, but it's always there to ponder and to inspire.

We see a world around us that has inconsistent respect for human rights and requires increasingly self-imposed responsibilities for the welfare of others. The rising tide of interdependency raises questions about the increasing need for a global ethic. I appreciate a statement prepared for the Second United Nations Conference on Human Settlements in June of 1996:

> Our challenge is to redesign and develop communities around universal principles—including love, honesty, moderation, humility, hospitality, justice and unity—which promote social cohesion, and without which no community, no matter how economically prosperous, intellectually endowed or technologically advanced, can long endure.[4]

---

4    Statement by the Bahá'í International Community, Office of Public Affairs, Paris

It's worth paraphrasing that last quote: "Our challenge is ... to develop communities around universal principles ... without which no community, no matter how economically, intellectually or technologically advanced, can long endure."

The assurance of our prosperous future comes in each of us individually practicing trust-building ethics that support universal principles afforded every human being on the planet. That's the clarion call at the third step of the moral ladder: *"It's About All of Us."*

### "Say Goodbye, Grace"

As Grace reads my *Noble Nine*, she's seeing some of them as relevant and others as a bit distant.

"They definitely take work, practice and belief," I remind her. "How about this. You pick three that you think you can more easily master, watch the results and get back to me."

"Which three?" she's asking.

"Which ones resonate with you, Grace?"

Looks like she's going with using the *Ethical Acid Tests* as she makes her choices; those seem clear to her. She's also going to try practicing Behindism so she can cast a different light on her choices. And for her third?

She's telling me to choose.

"Nuh-uh, Grace. These are like trying on new clothes. It's about what makes you feel the best."

She'll go with *Ladder up!* She says it's close to Behindism, and she's already read this book, too, so it's a natural step.

"Nice pun, Grace." And with that, she's walking down her path. "Bye for now, Grace." Hmm, I don't think she heard me. Darn fictional characters!

If you're having trouble seeing relevance or picking your three, maybe I can remind you about *your* importance in choosing.

Many people today feel that life has lost meaning. They read the headlines, hear "alternative facts" (now, there's some coded language), see that honesty and integrity have become commodities and they are deflated. Life is a rose bush full of thorns.

Have we lost meaningful lives? I don't think so. We live lives far wealthier than the rulers, kings and queens of the past. There may be an incredible Rocco opulence to the life and palaces of Louis XIV and Marie Antoinette in the 1700s for instance. But I can assure you, they would give most of that up for instant hot water, indoor plumbing and heating, common sense personal hygiene, scientifically-based health care, transportation that accomplishes in minutes or hours what once took weeks or months, individual rights and freedoms, a world of laws and agreements and so much more that were non-existent then. These are signs of our social as well as our technological progress. The list is nearly endless.

I'm not suggesting these material things create a sense of purpose. Quite the opposite: I think the rise of our material-based world has added little to the meaning in our lives. What these advances have given us is the time, opportunity and resources to deepen our individual and collective understanding about what makes life meaningful or meaningless.

What's the key to meaningfulness? I believe it is the ability to trust one another as we strive to advance the quality of our lives. Trustworthiness gives meaning to our lives. If we can count on one another 100 percent of the time, we can achieve what we can imagine together. If we bend our decisions to please our lower natures, we can never attain our greatest ambitions. Our gift of free will can be used for good and for naught. Where we build trustworthiness, it is hard to use it for naught and easier to use it for good.

The connections we make with one another, the ethics we practice with one another, these will define the quality of our lives. I hope you'll look to the Noble Nine as mileposts along the path of that change. Whether you want to be a paradigm *Scout, Pioneer* or *Settler*, knowing progress is naturally rooted in our rational, emotional, physical and spiritual selves provides us a wonderful certainty. Indeed, we have the glorious capacities and conscious knowledge to live nobly and bring life to the understanding that there's no right way to do the wrong thing!

# EXPANDED DEFINITIONS

## *(from Chapter One)*

**<u>Morals</u> are the standards of an individual or group about what is right and what is wrong.** Morals are the good or right understanding in support of our actions. The very word "moral" comes from the Latin *moralis*, meaning "customs" or "manners." Our morals form the individual and group codes we use for making right and wrong choices.

**<u>Ethics</u> are an examination of right and wrong and the actions taken after that examination.** Ethics are related to personal character. The term comes from the Greek word *ethos* that actually means character. Ethics are defined by the actions people *ought* to take in pursuit of the right goals. Ethics also concentrate on examining human values through examination of their conduct.

**<u>Legality</u> (what is legal or illegal), comes from enforced social arrangements based on our morals.** Depending on your source, the word "legal" comes from late Middle English, from French or from the Latin, *legalis*, from *lex* or *leg*—as in, where do you stand?

**Moral Development is the continual growth of moral reasoning and moral capacity.** Dr. Lawrence Kohlberg and his associates at Harvard's Center for Moral Education identified three distinct levels and six stages of this development in 1976.

**Ethical Development is the progression of actions based on an increasingly selfless perspective in our decisions.** It includes utilizing an understanding of our progressive moral capacities to take on increasingly ethical actions.

# ETHICS PRINCIPLES SUMMARIZED

Throughout this book, you've seen statements summarizing the main ethical principles I covered along the way. I offer them here in a single list with chapter references for your review. I hope this summary will be helpful as you consider your own contribution to our progress toward a society where our decisions—individually and collectively—consistently consider the equity of the community, the greater good of the people around us and the progress of world we live in.

## The 21 Principles of Leading an Ethically Driven Life

1 Laws tell us what we can do; ethics tell us what we should do. *[Chapter 1]*

2 Transparency isn't always on the most ethical pathway, truth is. *[Chapter 2]*

**3** Questions with a listening ear will get you a lot closer to the truth than creating your own. *[Chapter 2]*

**4** Our ethics are expressed not in what we say, but by what we do. *[Chapter 3]*

**5** Being trusted is the foundation of our greatest personal freedoms. *[Chapter 3]*

**6** Ethical actions exercise our virtues, the most praiseworthy expressions of our higher natures. *[Chapter 4]*

**7** When we take on responsibility for our future generations, it is a selfless act fulfilling our spiritual desire to carry forward an ever-advancing civilization. *[Chapter 4]*

**8** Ethics are in the walking, not the talking! *[Chapter 5]*

**9** Ethics are best understood when they are personalized. *[Chapter 5]*

**10** Knowledge is not wisdom; how you use your knowledge is an indicator of your wisdom. And what bridges the gap between your knowledge and your wisdom are your ethics. *[Chapter 5]*

**11** With paradigms, a truer truth always wins! *[Chapter 6]*

**12** The capital T-Truth is that moral standards are universal; that's what makes them moral, and our actions are either ethical or unethical on that universal basis. *[Chapter 7]*

**13** Allowances must be made as we weigh our ethical choices for our emotional and spiritual gains and losses. *[Chapter 8]*

**14** If what is ethical for one group is not ethical for another, but interactions between the two ignore the difference, then ethical relativism deeply shades any hope of universal rights in both groups. *[Chapter 10]*

**15** Trustworthiness leaves little room for relativism. *[Chapter 10]*

**16** What is moral is not simply what is accepted, but what a person of good character understands is appropriate on a universal basis. *[Chapter 11]*

**17** Moral frameworks and justifications that ignore the real victims of our unethical choices enable us to feel ethical while making the wrong choices. *[Chapter 12]*

**18** We have the capacity to make ethical choices from an ever-advancing, virtue-driven set of humane values guided by our moral development and chosen through an exercise of our higher nature-driven, free will. *[Chapter 13]*

**19** If we are honest with our words, we will see the truth of our actions. *[Chapter 14]*

**20** If our action will not create trust or enhance our trustworthiness or the respect of others, it is neither planned nor executed. *[Chapter 14]*

**21** Ethics are based on an exercise of our virtues, not an exercise of our rights. *[Chapter 16]*

# About The Author

Dr. Christopher Gilbert, author of the best-selling book *There's No Right Way to Do the Wrong Thing,* is a senior international ethics consultant and popular keynote speaker. As co-founder of NobleEdge Consulting (www. nobleedgeconsulting.com), he has worked with Fortune 500, government, and non-profit organizations, including the Bill and Melinda Gates Foundation, traveling the globe to spearhead sustainability, human capacity development and business conduct programs.

Chris has been a contributing author to CNBC, Fox News, Entrepreneur, Quartz, Hitched, Yahoo Finance, Retail Dive, Young Upstarts, and Successful Business News. He has also been a featured guest on worldwide Podcasts and nationally syndicated radio shows.

With over 25 years of teaching experience in colleges and universities on four continents, Chris has also pioneered nationally recognized professional development and ethics centers.

As a motivational speaker and author, he is well known for his informative humor, authenticity and personalized inspiration. He holds a Ph.D. specializing in leadership ethics, an MBA and a B.S. in Geology.

When he's not traveling for work, Chris spends his time as a volunteer in an inter-faith organization fighting homelessness in his community. He has also served two terms as Pierce County Ethics Commissioner in Washington State.

Chris is privileged to split the remaining ten minutes of his spare time between his daughters and grandchildren, community theater and gourmet cooking adventures with his wife, Marie, (including an authentic re-creation of Titanic's last first class eleven-course dinner). He and his family are blessed to live and sail on the beautiful estuarian waters of the Salish Sea outside Seattle, Washington.

# Contact Information

## WORKSHOPS, PRESENTATIONS AND TRAININGS

D r. Christopher Gilbert facilitates cutting-edge ethics and business conduct workshops and provides keynotes and presentations locally and globally. He also leads highly successful strategic planning and team building retreats.

If you would like to engage him for your next event or learn more about NobleEdge's leading workshops including *The You Turn: From Conflict to Collaboration*, and *There's No Right Way to Do the Wrong Thing*, contact:

Info@NobleEdgeConsulting.com
+1 (253) 225-2272
www.NobleEdgeConsulting.com

**Twitter**: @EthicsRUs
**LinkedIn**: Christopher Gilbert
**LinkedIn**: NobleEdge Consulting
**Facebook**: NobleEdge Consulting

Write to us with your comments, questions,
or your own ethics tales to:
Dr. Christopher Gilbert
NobleEdge Consulting
P.O. Box 975
Wauna, WA 98395

# A free ebook edition
# is available with the
# purchase of this book.

**To claim your free ebook edition:**

1. Visit MorganJamesBOGO.com
2. Sign your name CLEARLY in the space
3. Complete the form and submit a photo of the entire copyright page
4. You or your friend can download the ebook to your preferred device

## Print & Digital Together Forever.

Snap a photo    Free ebook    Read anywhere

CPSIA information can be obtained
at www.ICGtesting.com
Printed in the USA
JSHW030006100721
16779JS00002B/84

9 781631 954054